Praise for *Collective Lea*

In this excellent book, Peter DeWitt demonstrates how instructional leadership teams can have a greater impact on student learning. Offering a balance between research and practice, DeWitt shows, for example, how the mindsets both of individuals and of their teams can help them meet challenges and achieve that impact. As an experienced teacher, principal, worldwide consultant, and writer, DeWitt speaks with authority and wisdom.

—Carol Dweck, Lewis & Virginia Eaton Professor of Psychology
Department of Psychology
Stanford University
Stanford, CA

Collective efficacy has a powerful impact on leaders, teachers, and students, but it is hard to implement. DeWitt teases out the key skillsets and mindsets needed: understanding one another, collaborating, and evaluating impact. He addresses the critics and shows more than a correlation of successful students and teachers; DeWitt proves that actively implementing a culture of collective efficacy leads to higher levels of satisfaction, greater impact on students, and successful implementation across the school. This is not only a "how to" book, but it also is grounded firmly in evidence and is a pleasure to read.

—John Hattie, Emeritus Laureate Professor
Melbourne Graduate School of Education
Author, *Visible Learning*
Melbourne, Victoria
Australia

Insightful and practical—this book is a must read for formal and informal school leaders as well as leadership teams who aspire to improve outcomes for all students. DeWitt combines research and field experience in order to demonstrate specific ways to strengthen commitment, collaboration, and confidence among members of leadership teams in schools. This book is timely, relevant, and an important contribution to the literature on collective efficacy.

—Jenni Donohoo, Provincial Literacy Lead
Council of Ontario Directors of Education
Author, *Collective Efficacy*

Instructional leadership teams play a vital role in supporting learning in schools. They are especially important during this time of rapidly changing expectations. In this book, Peter DeWitt applies the theory of collective efficacy to these instructional leadership teams, outlining eight important contributors. Including student councils as part of a school's leadership is a fresh new approach.

—Megan Tschannen-Moran, Professor of Educational Leadership
William & Mary School of Education
Williamsburg, VA

This book will challenge leaders and make a difference for children. It offers a pragmatic, research-based approach to building the collective efficacy of leaders in all roles in a school with intention and commitment to relationship building, collaboration, data collection, and action research toward measurable outcomes.

The pandemic pivot highlighted the need for collective leader efficacy as foundational and essential in responding to the changing parameters and dynamics of our new reality in education. It will likely never look the same and this is the right focus at the perfect time.

The skills are built toward the development of a theory of action model logically and on the shoulders of great practitioners and scholars. The learning, digesting, and applying to practice model is transformative.

The contributors to CLE are clear and built on the foundation of mindset and well-being. In that environment, the other contributors are enhanced.

—Janice White, Associate Professor
Esteves School of Education
Russell Sage College
Troy, NY

DeWitt straddles the ground between collective efficacy, instructional leadership, and distributed leadership. The book is packed to the rafters with practical exercises, tools, and protocols that will help you to get (meaningfully) busy at enhancing the learning lives and well-being of children. You will not be handed silver bullets or magic beans, but you will find much to support deep impact.

—Arran Hamilton, Group Director, Education
Cognition Education Ltd.
Kuala Lumpur, Malaysia

We have known for quite some time that collective teacher efficacy is a powerful influence on student learning. Before we can expect teachers to focus on building their capability though, we first need school leaders and leadership teams that believe that: 1) this is possible; 2) it is their responsibility to nurture; and 3) they have the skills and capabilities to do so. Put simply, we need Collective Leader Efficacy! In this book, Peter DeWitt draws upon research and personal practice to create a compelling narrative in support of deliberately and intentionally building collective leader efficacy (CLE). This is a book I will be both referring to and recommending to colleagues well into the future.

—Timothy O'Leary, Former School Leader
Education Consultant

As a researcher and academic and experienced school leader, DeWitt offers a refreshing approach and insight into leadership in schools. The structure of the chapters takes you on the journey of learning and experience and always draws it back to key questions/reflections and actionable steps.

DeWitt presents models in clear language to meet all busy school leaders. He gets it. He understands the complexities and multiple relationships in schools. This book is highly suitable for any school leader in any country. Many leadership books can leave you inspired but with no idea or time to apply it. This book is different—you will be inspired and empowered to leave with strategies, models, and activities that actually work!

—Anne-Marie Duguid, Director
Empowering Education Partnership
London, UK

Collective leader efficacy is a new concept that Peter proposes to consider how leadership teams can work together to make a difference in the lives of students. While there are many books on the nature and change of school leadership, this book makes a difference with its practitioner-oriented approach. Not only does it propose a new concept that extends our thinking on leadership towards its collective impact, but it sets out the individual dimensions that shape this practice in a very practical way. For each dimension that contributes to collective leader efficacy, it lays out the theory of change, provides bibliographical resources, guiding questions and activities that educational leaders can use to reflect on how to improve their practice. A very practical resource for educational leaders internationally which is valuable in the current times of uncertainty and change.

—Beatriz Pont, Senior Education Policy Analyst
OECD Directorate for Education and Skills
Paris, France

Collective Leader Efficacy

To Doug. I hope you read this one!
To Marilyn (1931-2021). We will miss the rides through Waterville,
but mostly we'll just miss our time with you.

Collective Leader Efficacy

Strengthening Instructional Leadership Teams

Peter M. DeWitt

Foreword by Michael Fullan

A Joint Publication

FOR INFORMATION:

Corwin

A SAGE Company

2455 Teller Road

Thousand Oaks, California 91320

(800) 233-9936

www.corwin.com

SAGE Publications Ltd.

1 Oliver's Yard

55 City Road

London EC1Y 1SP

United Kingdom

SAGE Publications India Pvt. Ltd.

B 1/I 1 Mohan Cooperative Industrial Area

Mathura Road, New Delhi 110 044

India

SAGE Publications Asia-Pacific Pte. Ltd.

18 Cross Street #10-10/11/12

China Square Central

Singapore 048423

President: Mike Soules

Associate Vice President and
  Editorial Director: Monica Eckman

Senior Acquisitions Editor: Ariel Curry

Senior Content Development
  Editor: Desirée A. Bartlett

Senior Editorial
  Assistant: Caroline Timmings

Project Editor: Amy Schroller

Copy Editor: Erin Livingston

Typesetter: C&M Digitals (P) Ltd.

Proofreader: Larry Baker

Cover Designer: Gail Buschman

Marketing Manager: Morgan Fox

Printed in the United States of America

Library of Congress Cataloging-in-Publication Data

Names: DeWitt, Peter M., author.

Title: Collective leader efficacy : strengthening the impact of instructional leadership teams / Peter M. DeWitt.

Description: Thousand Oaks, California : Corwin, [2022] | Includes bibliographical references and index.

Identifiers: LCCN 2021020812 | ISBN 9781071813720 (paperback) | ISBN 9781071813768 (epub) | ISBN 9781071813751 (epub) | ISBN 9781071813744 (pdf)

Subjects: LCSH: Teaching teams. | Educational leadership.

Classification: LCC LB1029.T4 D49 2022 | DDC 371.14/8—dc23

LC record available at https://lccn.loc.gov/2021020812

This book is printed on acid-free paper.

21 22 23 24 25 10 9 8 7 6 5 4 3 2

CONTENTS

FOREWORD

Believe it or not, no one has singled out collective *leader* efficacy. We can find lots about collective efficacy and about leader efficacy but nothing that systematically brings them together as a single unified phenomenon. Peter DeWitt is not on top of his field so much as he is constantly *immersed* in it. He cycles in and around hosting sessions, managing and writing blogs, participating in action, cultivating and publishing the work of others, and writing his own books. He is knowledgeable to the minute in a field that is always changing.

In such a dynamic domain, Peter is the ideal person for consolidating what we know, as he formulates guiding questions for what we should still be seeking to know. DeWitt organizes the challenge of leadership around eight stimulating themes (such as context beliefs, skills, confidence, and a focus on improvement). He offers readers valuable insights in each area but also challenges us with new questions—the net effect is a sensation of questioning, learning, consolidating, and new questions. There is a learning framework common to each chapter: a theory of action focused on the theme in the chapter followed by a set of guiding questions. The sensation one gets is of constantly learning new things, consolidating the learning through guiding questions, and then, just as things settle, along comes the next chapter and corresponding additional questions.

By engaging the reader in new stimuli and related knowledge building, the net effect is a growing sense of the core of leader efficacy. This core is centered around four key questions: How are students and teachers working together to create authentic learning experiences? How are we supporting students and teachers in that process? How do we engage families in the process? And what unbiased evidence do we collect to understand our impact? The book itself is full of leading questions—that is, questions and ideas arising from the material. When these responses are not only connected back to the particular questions but also can be compared across sets of questions, then the readers begin to consolidate and learn the nuances of how to combine the eight key contributors of integrating teacher and leadership efficacy in a single enterprise.

Collective Leader Efficacy does not hand the reader the answers on a platter. But by joining leader and collective efficacy into a single concept, the ideas lead the reader to a single domain, namely this: How do leader and group functioning merge to provide impactful learning as both caused by and appreciated by students, parents, teachers, and formal leaders within? Each of the chapters provides a theory of action along with guiding questions designed to inform readers' thinking and actions. In this way, readers will find themselves continuously drawn into the process of developmental thinking and action.

Collective Leader Efficacy is a book that makes you think; it rewards the reader with directional questions and answers that can be applied as new learnings are consolidated. As more and more books appear on efficacy, it is essential for us to figure out how leadership is best understood. This book will help the reader do just that.

—Michael Fullan, Author, Speaker, Educational Consultant
Global Leadership Director, New Pedagogies for Deep Learning
Former Dean and Professor Emeritus, University of Toronto

ACKNOWLEDGMENTS

During the year of COVID, when I sat down to write this book, I watched family and friends experience major health issues, had good friends who are business owners come close to losing their businesses every single week, lost someone very close to me due to COVID, and watched eye-opening news reports that will forever change us. Although I have always felt fortunate to be surrounded by a supportive and loving family as well as really good friends, this past year was clearly one where those in our lives mattered more than ever. I would like to thank everyone for their love and support, but there are a few who stand out.

Thank you to my partner, Doug; my mom; and my family, especially to my sister Trish and brother Frank, who took on some major health issues in the last year and came out swinging. You both were inspirational. To John Hattie, Jenni Donohoo, and Michael Fullan for your guidance and willingness to always lend your support. Janice White and Kenneth Leithwood also gave me critical feedback that was important to the development of this book. I would like to thank Alison Mitchell, Madelaine Baker, Ray Boyd, Ann-Marie Duguid, and Julian Drinkall for their vignettes in this book outlining what certain drivers of collective leader efficacy look like in practice.

Thank you to Elizabeth Rich, my friend and editor from *Education Week*, for giving me the space to engage in some very deep, and sometimes difficult, conversations on A Seat at the Table. To Linda Kindlon and Justin Cary for being a model for waking up every morning and reinventing yourselves in order to keep living your dreams. I will wash dishes, box up sweets, and deliver to cars in the parking lot any time. To Peter Slattery and Peter Mesh, not only for your cool names but also for being role models to so many. And to Helen Butler, Michael Mago, and Anne Wilkins for never letting an ocean and many time zones ever get in the way of friendship.

Lastly, thank you to my Corwin team: Ariel Curry for supporting me on this book and for co-creating our Leaders Coaching Leaders podcast, Morgan Fox, Sharon Pendergast, and Desirée Bartlett for your support while writing this book.

ABOUT THE AUTHOR

Photo by Albert J. Gnidica

Peter M. DeWitt, EdD is a former K-5 teacher (11 years) and principal (eight years). He is a school leadership coach who runs competency-based workshops and courses and provides keynotes nationally and internationally. DeWitt works with K-12 school leaders and aspiring school leaders on instructional leadership, creating collaborative cultures, fostering school climates, and developing impactful school leadership teams.

His work has been adopted at the state and university levels, and he works with numerous school districts, school boards, regional networks, and ministries of education around North America, Australia, Asia, Europe, the Middle East, and the United Kingdom.

Peter writes the Finding Common Ground column for *Education Week*, which has been in circulation since 2011. In 2020, DeWitt co-created *Education Week*'s A Seat at the Table with his editor Elizabeth Rich, in which he moderates conversations with experts focusing on race, equity, ethics, gender, sexual orientation, research, trauma, and many other educational topics. In 2021, he and Corwin editor Ariel Curry began co-hosting the Leaders Coaching Leaders podcast.

Additionally, DeWitt is the series editor for the Connected Educator Series (Corwin) and the Impact Series (Corwin) that include books by Viviane Robinson, Andy Hargreaves, Pasi Sahlberg, Yong Zhao, and Michael Fullan. He is the 2013 School Administrators Association of New York State's (SAANYS) Outstanding Educator of the Year.

Peter is the author, co-author, or contributor of numerous books:

- *Dignity for All: Safeguarding LGBT Students* (Corwin, 2012)

- *School Climate Change* (Association of Supervision and Curriculum Development, co-authored with Sean Slade, 2014)

- *Flipping Leadership Doesn't Mean Reinventing the Wheel* (Corwin, 2014)

- *Collaborative Leadership: Six Influences That Matter Most* (Corwin/Learning Forward, 2016)

- *School Climate: Leading With Collective Teacher Efficacy* (Corwin/Ontario Principals' Council, 2017)

- *Coach It Further: Using the Art of Coaching to Improve School Leadership* (Corwin, 2018)

- *Instructional Leadership: Creating Practice Out of Theory* (Corwin, 2020)

- *10 Mindframes for Leaders: The Why, How, and What of the Visible Learning Leader* (Corwin, edited by John Hattie, 2020)

Peter's articles have appeared in educational research journals at the state, national, and international levels. He has presented at forums and conferences at state, national, and international levels. His articles and books have been translated into different languages.

Peter has worked with many state, national, and international organizations, including the American Association of School Administrators (AASA); numerous authorities around Canada; Victoria Department of Education (Australia), Cognition Education; OSIRIS Education in the UK; University of Rotterdam (Netherlands); Kuwait Technical College; the New York City Department of Education Universal Literacy Program; Texas Association of School Administrators (TASA); the National Education Association (NEA); the National Association of Secondary School Principals (NASSP); the National Association of School Psychologists; the Association of Supervision and Curriculum Development (ASCD); l'Association des directions et directions adjointes des écoles franco-ontariennes (ADFO); the Catholic Principals' Council of Ontario (CPCO); the Ontario Principals' Council (OPC); National School Climate Center; and GLSEN, PBS, NPR, ABC, and NBC's Education Nation, where he sat on a school safety panel with Hoda Kotb and Goldie Hawn.

VOCABULARY TERMS

To create a more uniform and inclusive reading experience and a common language and common understanding for all readers, I define the following terms up front.

Collaborative leadership: Describes a type of leadership in which those in a leadership position take purposeful actions to enhance the instruction of teachers, build deep relationships with all stakeholders through understanding self-efficacy, and build collective efficacy to deepen learning together.

Department chair (or head): A leadership position held by a faculty member in a given content area, particularly in middle and secondary schools. Department heads are sometimes responsible for learning walks and facilitating curricular discussions. They sometimes mentor new teachers within their department.

Deputy head: A teacher or leader who is second in charge behind a head teacher. The parallel position in the United States is an assistant principal or vice principal.

Distributed leadership: Describes a type of leadership in which the leadership team, made up of various members of a school, distribute the work so it doesn't fall on the shoulders of one person.

Head teacher: In the United Kingdom, the head teacher is also referred to as the *school director*. The position represents those leaders with the most responsibility in a school. The parallel position in the United States and Canada is the building principal.

Instructional coach: An individual who works with a teacher or group of teachers on their instructional practices. Instructional coaches take teachers through coaching cycles in which they focus on evidence-based practices and look for improvement. Instructional coaches can be full-time positions, but due to budget constraints, instructional coaches may also work half-time as a classroom teacher and half-time as an instructional coach, particularly in middle schools and secondary schools where school days are broken up into formal periods.

Instructional leadership: Describes a type of leadership in which those in a leadership position focus their efforts on the implementation of practices that will positively impact student learning.

Learning specialists: Highly skilled classroom teachers who want to remain in the classroom but also help out colleagues who want to improve their practices.

Middle manager: A school building leader who reports to a greater authority; for example, to district-level leaders (in the United States). At the school site, the school building leader has a staff that reports to them. This makes them middle managers.

PLC leads: Professional learning community (PLC) leads are responsible for facilitating discussions with the PLC, usually focused on a communities-of-practice approach within a grade level or department. They organize and lead discussions on curriculum, grading, and other student needs.

School building leader: An individual who is responsible for leading a primary, middle, or secondary school or any combination of these (such as PreK–8 buildings). Terms such as *school administrator* have also been used for this position.

School divisions/school boards: Canada is quite unique in the world in that they do not have an education department at the national level. There are 13 different jurisdictions in the country to represent 10 provinces and three territories, and they are individually responsible for their own education systems. School divisions and school boards include primary and secondary schools within their area. The parallel divisions in the United States are school districts.

Systems leadership: Clive Dimmock (2016) says, "If we take the school (meso level) as the system, then the head teacher is a system leader." In the United States, systems leadership would be an assistant superintendent or superintendent because most school buildings are housed in school districts. A school district would be the overall system.

WHAT YOU NEED TO KNOW

I will use these vocabulary terms throughout the book. Although it is nearly impossible to align terms due to their various job duties, I believe these terms are the most positive and inclusive way to move forward.

School building leader: This term will be used for head teachers, school principals, school directors, or system leaders.

Assistant principal: This term will be used for deputy heads or vice principals.

Teacher leader: This term will be used for department chairs, grade-level chairs, and PLC leads.

INTRODUCTION

What has been your experience with instructional leadership teams (ILTs), school planning teams, or shared decision-making teams? Have they been positive experiences in which you learned a great deal about student and adult learning? In your experience, are they collaborative sessions in which ideas are shared and fostered? Have they helped you learn more about yourself? Or have they been a colossal waste of time that you can only dream of ever getting back?

As a teacher, I was on a few building-level teams, all with different names, but none of them were intentionally focused on teaching and learning. Mostly they focused on communication with families, which is important, or management of the building, which is also important. However, none of them focused on learning, which seems odd to me, considering that we work in schools, where you'd think the primary focus should be on learning. Many times, my role was to be present at the meetings and so I defaulted to agreeing with the school leader.

As a school building leader, I helped develop a school leadership team; although we agreed that we would only focus on activities that would improve our school climate, we did not always discuss teaching and learning. Over time, however, we began to make that more and more of our focus. Upon reflection, I wish we could go back and create a process of inquiry that was more defined, elevate the voices a bit more, and create new roles that tapped into a given individual's creativity, but overall, our discourse added to our development as a school leadership team.

This book is about how school building leaders can work with their collective leadership teams to have a deeper impact on student learning, tap into the leadership of others who are a part of the collective, and define a focus that can positively impact the school community. Regardless of whether the teams have been called *shared decision-making teams*, *school planning teams*, or *building-level teams*, this book will take you through a process to help you re-energize those teams and help them be more impactful when it comes to student learning.

I know what you're thinking: *Yet another book on school leadership teams*. Here's the thing: This is different because this book is about a balance between the research we need to know about instruction and leadership and the drivers necessary to build an impactful team. It is also about the inquiry process that so many teams desperately need to go through to create a community of learners in their schools. As we focus on the nuances of instruction and teamwork, we are building the case for developing collective leader efficacy.

Hattie et al. (2020) explain that collective efficacy is the shared conviction that educators make a significant contribution in raising student achievement. Self-efficacy and collective efficacy are so much more than whether a person or team has confidence or not. Bandura (1997) found that there are four experiences that impact efficacy in positive ways.

- **Mastery experiences:** Bandra says, "Successes build a robust belief in one's personal efficacy. Failures undermine it, especially if failures occur before a sense of efficacy is firmly established. If people experience only easy successes, they come to expect only easy successes, they come to expect quick results and are easily discouraged by failure" (p. 80). Mastery experiences come from those challenging situations where we did not give up and came out successfully on the other side.

- **Vicarious experiences:** Bandura writes, "Seeing or visualizing people similar to oneself perform successfully typically raises efficacy beliefs in observers that they themselves possess the capabilities to master comparable activities" (p. 87).

- **Social persuasion:** Bandura explains, "It is easier to sustain a sense of efficacy, especially when struggling with difficulties, if significant others express faith in one's capabilities than if they convey doubts" (p. 101).

- **Affective states:** Bandura writes, "The fourth major way of altering efficacy beliefs is to enhance physical status, reduce stress levels and negative emotional proclivities, and correct misinterpretations of bodily states" (p. 106). What we know is that anxiety diminishes efficacy and excitement increases it. Bringing curiosity and voice to our ILTs can help create positive affective states.

As we can see from these four experiences, raising the efficacy of individuals or a team takes modeling, planning, challenging each other's thinking, and having the ability to drop whatever status we may have based on our position and focus on raising the status of those sitting around the table. It takes an understanding of how we communicate with each other and how our communication impacts the people around the table.

Additionally, when it comes to building the collective efficacy of a team, we have to develop a deep understanding of student learning and of what our students need when it comes to social-emotional and academic learning. What we know is that collective efficacy is about how we come together as a team, and there is always so much potential in what teams can do together.

> Collective leader efficacy is the shared conviction that a school's ILT can make a significant contribution in raising student achievement.

Uniting teams and reaching our full potential as a team with a focus strictly on student learning is not easily done because over the last few decades, we have all seen an increase in accountability, destructive rhetoric about the state of education in many countries, teacher strikes due to low wages and a lack of resources, institutional discrimination and racism, cuts to school district and division budgets that have resulted in teacher and school leader layoffs, and destruction of programs. On top of all of that, we recently experienced a devastating pandemic that (at the beginning) put 85% of the world's population of students in some sort of remote learning situation (UNESCO, 2021).

While these challenges seem daunting, we also understand that they are some of the very reasons why school leadership teams are more important than ever. Schools have real issues that need real solutions, and they need to rebuild and reboot the work they were doing prior to the pandemic while learning from it in order to build back stronger than before. What makes solving these issues very difficult is that there are individuals within schools who may actually be contributing to the problem and not the solution.

THE PROMISE OF COLLECTIVE LEADER EFFICACY

As much as I believe that collective efficacy is a phenomenon that is worth our time, there is one aspect to it that has concerned me over the past few years. Research shows that collective efficacy was three times more likely to contribute to student achievement than any other influences on learning (Hattie, 2016). Collective efficacy and student achievement have a reciprocal benefit, meaning that sometimes we contribute to the success of others and at other times, others contribute to our success.

Collective efficacy has many levels of importance beyond the impact on student achievement. Collective efficacy is about fostering leadership, independence, and interdependence among teachers, and it is also about elevating the power of the collective. School leaders need to engage in joint work with teachers and staff within their schools that involves inquiry cycles of learning if they are to have a true impact on student learning. What we also know is that collaborative groups such as PLCs are popular in schools, but many teachers see PLCs as contrived collaboration (Hargreaves & O'Connor, 2018b) because although PLCs are comprised of teachers, those same teachers do not feel they have a voice in what they focus on. They have no shared conviction and are not truly engaged in joint work.

What we need to look at is how to strengthen the ingredients of more impactful school teams, given their most critical issues, and develop a process that contributes to the shared conviction so those teams can have more of a positive impact on student learning.

To be more effective, the ILT needs to understand the crucial elements of the process of developing collective leader efficacy. It takes establishing a diverse ILT, charting the course through academic and social-emotional needs, and building trust among individuals on the team, and then establishing trust between the team and the school community. Only then will the ILT have a positive impact. The process also involves understanding what it's like to be a part of a system. Clive Dimmock (2016) writes,

> The level at which we think about a system is important for understanding system leadership in its contemporary context. If we take the school (meso level) as the system, then the head teacher is a system leader. However, if we consider the local authority or the nation as the system (macro level), then the head teacher of a school becomes leader of a sub-system, and to be a system leader, s(he) must contribute to the greater good of other schools beyond their own. (p. 63)

For school leadership teams to have an impact and develop a shared conviction, they need to consider the following key components:

- **drivers for improvement.** In this book, there are eight specific drivers that contribute to the success of school leadership teams, which will then help the team develop collective leader efficacy;

- a **focus** for the improvement, which involves a focus on learning;

- and finally, a **process,** such as developing a cycle of inquiry.

Michael Fullan (2011) writes that drivers "are those policy and strategy levers that have the least and best chance of driving successful reform." Taking Fullan's extensive work on drivers into consideration, and the need to inspire collective work through our ILTs, there are eight specific drivers necessary to develop collective leader efficacy.

In Section II, you will learn about mindset, context beliefs, the skills to work in collectives, and a few other drivers that are specific to fostering collective leader efficacy. Drivers are those areas we need to think about when developing our team and as we work with our team. This book, and the research within it, is about improving beliefs and actions and then understanding how they intersect to create more functional, and much more effective, school leadership teams.

The focus of the ILT is the instructional core of their building. In other words, why should students enter your school? Are they engaged or merely showing up? Do they have a voice in their own learning or are they only there to watch the adults work? What about marginalized students? Are they part of the instructional focus or do the adults have a deficit mindset where those students are concerned?

To do this work, school teams need to engage in a process of improvement, which is a cycle of inquiry in which teams develop purpose statements, inquiry questions, and a theory of action.

HOW TO APPROACH THIS BOOK

This is a guidebook, which means that whether you are in an ILT or you are a school building leader, readers need to be prepared to do work while reading. One of the drivers I lay out in this book is professional learning and development. Your team can use this book for their own professional learning and development as they offer professional learning and development to their colleagues.

I do not claim to have the answers to your issues, but I am hoping that through my words, the research, and the process that I lay out we develop a partnership in which your team can use these actionable steps to develop better questions and deeper practices. Collective leader efficacy is a process that needs to be developed, which is why this book is divided into three sections.

Section I will focus on the collective leader efficacy research. Section II will focus on eight drivers necessary to foster collective leader efficacy. These chapters will be much shorter because most of the chapters will only focus on one driver at a time.

Section III focuses on practice. It involves a cycle of inquiry. Your team will be asked to develop purpose statements, inquiry questions, and a theory of action. This section is completely hands-on, so be prepared to engage in the work.

FEATURES

Throughout this book, you will find recurring features that will help you engage with the material. These features are particularly useful to address as a team working through the book together.

▶ **Quotes:** Each chapter begins with a quote that serves as a teaser to the content of the chapter.

▶ **Theory of action:** Each chapter begins with a theory of action, which helps readers understand the reason for focusing our efforts on the content of the chapter.

▶ **Reflect:** These reflection prompts will help you process the information and the actions you will need to take.

▶ **Student council reflections:** Ideally, student voice is included in leadership-level conversations about student learning. Throughout this book, you will find student council reflections that ask you to consider how the work of collective efficacy can look at the student leadership level.

▶ **Note pages:** I have set aside blank sections for you to take notes as you read the book. These will prompt you to jot down your thoughts so that you can reread them when you revisit the book in the future.

▶ **Activities:** Engage in learning walks, SWOT analyses, and choosing roles on your team.

▶ **Tools of implementation:** Section III of the book focuses on developing a theory of action with your ILT; there you will find the cycle of inquiry tool as well as sample program logic models, which will help you define your team's desired outcomes and the steps necessary to achieve those outcomes.

> **Guiding questions:** For individuals, book clubs, professional learning communities (PLCs), and university classes, these questions appear at the beginning and end of each chapter to prompt your thinking and guide your discussions.

The purpose of this book is to offer research and practice opportunities that will help your team engage in open and honest conversations about your school's current reality. This is not a book that gives leaders and teams a few easy steps to improvement. We know those do not work because we are human, and we have flaws and emotions that can sometimes prevent us from moving forward. I'm asking you to be as reflective, honest, and open as you possibly can, because that will provide a safe space for the ILT to thrive and develop that shared conviction that is so badly needed these days.

Activity 0.1 SWOT Analysis
Your Team

Before we can engage in the work as a team, we need to understand our current reality as a team. This SWOT activity should be completed as a group to gain an understanding of your team's strengths, weaknesses, opportunities, and threats. Consider the following:

- **Strengths:** What are the strengths of your present team?

- **Weakness:** Where would you like to improve as a team?

- **Opportunities:** What opportunities are you open to engaging in?

- **Threats:** What threats compromise your team right now?

Write down your insights for each question.

(Continued)

SWOT ANALYSIS: YOUR TEAM

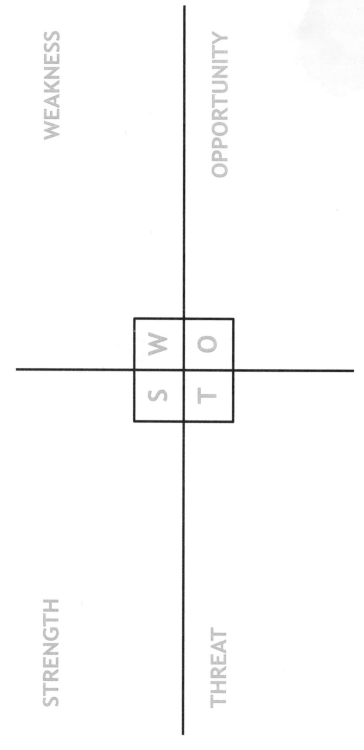

STRENGTH

WEAKNESS

THREAT

OPPORTUNITY

S | W
T | O

(Continued)

SECTION I

RESEARCH

Chapter 1: Collective Leader Efficacy

COLLECTIVE LEADER EFFICACY

I realize increasingly that I am only interested in learnings which significantly influence behavior.

Carl Rogers (1954)

THEORY OF ACTION

If . . . teams understand the research behind collective efficacy, then . . . they will be able to engage in a process that will increase the likelihood that they will develop it among their instructional leadership team.

GUIDING QUESTIONS

- What is social cognitive theory and why does it matter to the work we do in schools?

- Why does someone who has self-efficacy in one situation not have it in another?

- How does the research focusing on self-efficacy explain some of the difficult situations we find ourselves in as leaders?

- What is leadership efficacy and why does it explain the reason that some leaders so easily take on what others see as controversial issues?

- How might student councils be inspired by the work around self and collective efficacy?

- What is the cycle that needs to take place in order for collective teacher efficacy to be built?

- What is collective leader efficacy and why should it be a driver for school improvement?

WHAT IS COLLECTIVE LEADER EFFICACY?

Instructional leadership teams are collectives filled with individuals who bring a level of expertise to the table. That area of expertise varies depending on the individual's experience. Just as with our students, prior knowledge and background can enrich the learning experience. Think of Section I in this book as an opportunity to develop the mindfulness necessary to be a part of a collective. That collective, regardless of whether they have been referred to as *school planning teams*, shared *decision-making teams,* or *building-level teams,* needs to have a more impactful focus on learning. Throughout this book, I will refer to those teams as *instructional leadership teams* (ILTs).

ILTs are faced with the challenge of choosing where to lead their improvement. *Improvement* is such an interesting term. It is widely used in education and every other profession, but what does it mean to improve? Robinson (2018, p. 2) says, "To lead improvement is to exercise influence in ways that leave a team, organization, or system in a better state than before."

That focused improvement needs to be centered on learning. Too many school leadership teams fall apart because they lack this focus on learning. Develop a shared understanding of what it means to be a collective group and the research that supports that shared understanding. Ensure that the team has a shared commitment to doing the work.

Collective groups should

- create opportunities for reciprocal learning with one another,
- develop each other's leadership mindset,
- understand the necessity for a sense of well-being,
- develop each other's skill and confidence to work together as a collective, and
- develop strategies to create a positive impact on the school community.

The conversations needed to get to this point and then to the desired improvement are messy and take research. An ILT has enormous potential. I say that because as a school leader, the dialogue we engaged in as a team and the innovations we created together around learning had an enormous impact on our school community. The question is, can your school leadership team have a positive impact on student learning and reach their full potential? Studies on collective efficacy have shown only a moderate impact thus far. Does that mean we need to abandon this notion of building collective efficacy? I don't think it does. After all, many ILTs have a moderate impact at best; should we, therefore, abandon those leadership teams? No. There is great promise in those teams.

As a realist, I know that many ILTs do not reach their potential of impacting student learning because they don't see themselves as the drivers of improvement, haven't done the work to come together collectively as a team, and haven't pursued a process to really focus on improvement. Collective leader efficacy can only be collective leader efficacy when those necessary steps take place.

Recall Hattie et al.'s (2020) definition: "Collective efficacy is the shared conviction that educators make a significant contribution in raising student achievement." I co-authored that article with Donohoo and Hattie. The words we used are important and intentional. As educators responsible for the education of our students, I believe we should have a shared conviction. That shared conviction can help teams engage in more than a moderate impact.

However, I do not think that shared conviction stops with teachers, PLCs, or whatever the name of the collaboration they may be engaged in. I believe that shared conviction needs to extend to our school leadership teams. Given that, I believe collective leader efficacy is the shared conviction that a school's ILT can make a significant contribution in raising student achievement. That will only happen when those on the team see themselves as the drivers of improvement. Collective leader efficacy is developed when the leadership team works together, understands the complexities of working as a group, has confidence in each other's ability to improve the learning conditions for students, and develops the competence to do so. Unfortunately, too many school leadership teams fail (Barnett & McCormick, 2012) and never reach their full potential, which is why it's important to know how to develop collective leader efficacy among your ILT so the team doesn't meet that same fate and we can move past a moderate impact into a more profound one.

WHAT IS THE DIFFERENCE BETWEEN CLE AND CTE?

Barnett and McCormick (2012, pp. 669–670) found that "it is evident that the interplay of leadership and team processes characterized by dynamics and reciprocity underlie the development of critical team capabilities necessary for Senior Executive Leadership Team (aka. instructional leadership team) effectiveness." And that is what makes collective leader efficacy different from collective teacher efficacy.

Collective teacher efficacy involves groups of teachers. When teachers work together on a common goal, engage in different strategies to reach that goal, and collect evidence to understand their impact, then those teams of teachers typically hold common status, which means that no one teacher has more power than another. Collective leader efficacy is different because it involves at least one school building leader as well as teacher leaders and instructional coaches, and the building leader typically has more positional status than anyone else on the team; this creates a dynamic in which others on the team may not want to speak up and be seen as going against the wishes of their school building leader.

Additionally, the team itself is seen as having power because they are making decisions for the rest of the school community. Those on the team may enjoy the status of "being in the know" because they are on a school-based leadership team while others who are not on that team feel as if they are on the outside looking in and waiting for people to make decisions for them. Collective teacher efficacy does not often have that complicated interplay between a teacher and their evaluator (also known as their school building leader).

Tschannen-Moran and Barr (2004, p. 190) define *collective teacher efficacy* as "the collective self-perception that teachers in a given school make an educational difference to their students over and above the educational impact of their homes and communities." Critics suggest that this is not possible because those homes and communities have more of a profound impact on children than we are willing to admit. My concern with those criticisms is that we have students who come to us that lack equity of resources and experiences at home. Does that mean we should abandon those students? No, of course not. It takes a collective team to understand how to create the most inclusive learning environment for all students, regardless of their homes and communities. How else can we help those communities thrive?

In fact, in the introduction to this book, I cited Bandura's four experiences that increase efficacy. Bandura (1997) found that there are four experiences that impact efficacy in positive ways. Those four experiences are mastery experiences, vicarious experiences, social persuasion, and affective states. Bandura found that mastery experiences are the ones that offer us the most profound learning experiences and impact our efficacy the most because they tend to be the most difficult experiences we go through.

Our job as educators, regardless of whether we are engaged in our professional learning community (PLC) or participating in an ILT, is to educate all students, regardless of the home situations they come from; many times, those students who come from difficult situations have the potential to offer teams the best mastery experience as the team works to change the lives of those students for the better.

Collective teacher efficacy has the potential to positively impact grade levels and departments within a school, which is important. Grades and departments need to foster growth together, and empowering teachers through the process is beneficial for numerous reasons. Collective leader efficacy, though, has the potential to positively impact a whole building. It also tends to be a bit more of a complicated process because developing collective leader efficacy means that school building leaders are directly included in the process. Due to the school building leader's status mentioned above, other people on the ILT may consistently defer to the person they deem has the "power." Whenever possible, it is important for the school building leader to lower their status and raise the status of those around them by trying to soften the hierarchical structure that can be a barrier to improvement. (Invite your ILT to view Appendix 5 to see more about guiding questions concerning CLE and CTE.)

WHAT DRIVES IMPROVEMENT?

Through the work of the entire ILT, collective leader efficacy can be developed. A shared conviction can be possible. With the focus on learning, collective leader efficacy can be an important driver of school improvement. Fullan (2011) found that drivers "are those policy and strategy levers that have the least and best chance of driving successful reform" (p. 3).

Fullan (2011, p. 3) expands on the idea behind drivers for improvement:

> As an advance organizer, I suggest four criteria—all of which must be met in concert—which should be used for judging the likely effectiveness of a driver or set of drivers. Specifically, do the drivers, sooner than later,

1. foster intrinsic motivation of teachers and students,
2. engage educators and students in continuous improvement of instruction and learning,
3. inspire collective or team work, [and]
4. affect all teachers and students—100 percent?

When it comes to ILTs and developing collective leader efficacy, there are eight specific drivers that contribute to the success of the team. Those eight drivers make up Section II of this book. Unfortunately, many ILTs that are supposed to guide the mission and vision of a school do not always reach their full potential; they do not engage in behaviors and actions that fulfill the four criteria identified by Fullan. I certainly found myself on some of those teams when I was a teacher.

In an effort to use our past experiences to help drive our future endeavors, let's engage in some deliberate practice by reflecting on leadership teams you have been on in the past. How did they work? What did they focus on? Were they helpful or harmful to the school community? Take a moment to reflect.

REFLECT

Think about one of the leadership teams you have been a part of. If you have been on more than one, feel free to choose the best, the worst, or one that was somewhere in between and reflect on the following questions.

- What was the focus of the ILT?
- Did the ILT foster intrinsic motivation among teachers and students? If so, how?
- Did the ILT engage educators and students in continuous learning? If so, how?
- Did members of the team differentiate between opinions and facts while they sat together?
- Did the team inspire collective work or did only a few members do the work? Why did that happen?
- Did the work have a positive impact on all students and teachers? How do you know?
- What was the key ingredient to the teamwork? If there wasn't a key ingredient, what was missing?
- What did you learn from that process that you can take to the ILT you are working with now?

NOTES

Please take a moment to write down your thoughts, questions, and ideas.

When reflecting on these prompts, how often did you imagine the face of someone from your previous team who was difficult? How many times did you reflect on the improvement your team was trying to focus on but never achieved? Did it seem like everyone felt confident to be there? Or did some members seem to lack confidence? How often did you reflect on how great it can be to work within a social context at school?

TEAM IMPROVEMENT INVOLVES DEVELOPING SELF-EFFICACY

To have an impact on the school community, ILTs need to help develop the confidence of the team members. When individuals feel confident, they are more likely to try new activities, engage in deeper learning experiences, and perhaps be more open to learning from others as opposed to being defensive because they lack the confidence to engage in authentic reflective practices. Developing confidence begins with understanding the research behind self-efficacy. It means drilling down past the team and focusing on the individuals who make up the team.

Albert Bandura is accredited with the development of self-efficacy. It was based on his social cognitive theory, which, according to LaMorte (2019), "posits that learning occurs in a social context with a dynamic and reciprocal interaction of the person, environment, and behavior." School is the ultimate social context. Reciprocal interaction is key for your ILT.

Bandura (1997, p. 3) writes, "Self-efficacy refers to beliefs in one's capabilities to organize and execute the courses of action required to produce given attainments." This is often where individuals need to take time to differentiate some of the information. Having a belief in one's capabilities is a bit different from having the competency to carry them out. Bandura further states,

> Such beliefs influence the courses of action people choose to pursue, how much effort they put forth in given endeavors, how long they will persevere in the face of obstacles and failures, their resilience to adversity, whether their thought patterns are self-hindering or self-aiding, how much stress or depression they experience in coping with taxing environmental demands, and the level of accomplishments they realize. (p. 3)

STUDENT COUNCIL REFLECTION

Many schools have a student council. In some cases, that council is instrumental in school decision-making. Although student leadership groups lack the professional status and positional authority of collective leader teams, we can still ask how the research on collective efficacy applies at the student council level. Students should have a voice regarding decision-making that is focused on student learning. If you have a student council, ask the following questions:

- How do the students in the council develop each member's sense of self-efficacy?
- How do they build collective efficacy together?

Throughout the book, you will see opportunities to reflect on the role of student councils. If your school doesn't have a student council, read these reflections and put your thoughts in your back pocket for a later day.

TEAM IMPROVEMENT INVOLVES DEVELOPING LEADERSHIP SELF-EFFICACY

Like teachers, leaders can lack confidence. Leaders need to do the work of developing leadership self-efficacy. McCormick (2001) defines *leadership self-efficacy* as

> one's self-perceived capability to perform the cognitive and behavioral functions necessary to regulate group process in relation to goal achievement. . . . Put another way, it is a person's confidence in his or her ability to successfully lead a group. (p. 30)

Tschannen-Moran and Gareis (2007) write,

> Self-efficacy is task and context specific. A principal may feel efficacious for leading in particular contexts, but this self-efficacy may or may not transfer to other contexts, depending on the perceived similarities of the task and the context in which the task is undertaken. (p. 93)

School building leaders may have beliefs and a great deal of competence when it comes to certain situations, but those beliefs may not be exactly what the school community needs at that time. Or, worse than that, a school building leader may believe that they have the confidence to engage in instructional leadership, for example, but their actions do not support that belief. Individuals in the school might find the leader's actions to be nothing like the actions of a competent instructional leader. This is why the collective learning of any group is so important.

Bandura (2005, p. 307) says, "One cannot be all things, which would require mastery of every realm of human life." To extend the self-efficacy approach into a deeper level involving school leaders, Bandura (2000, p. 120) writes, "When faced with obstacles, setbacks, and failures, those who doubt their capabilities slacken their efforts, give up, or settle for mediocre solutions. Those who have a strong belief in the capabilities redouble their effort to master the challenge."

Tschannen-Moran and Gareis (2007, p. 91) write, "Principals with a low sense of self-efficacy have been found to perceive an inability to control their environment, and they tend to be less likely to identify appropriate strategies or modify unsuccessful ones." This enters into even more dangerous territory because Tschannen-Moran and Gareis follow up by writing, "When confronted with failure, they rigidly persist in their original course of action. When challenged, they are more likely to blame others."

Our efficacy can be enhanced by working in groups that help elevate it. When we join a group, we might enter with a low level of efficacy, but by working collaboratively, we can elevate our own sense of efficacy in a variety of situations. It's kind of like when we go for a run on our own—we may do three miles and feel tired every time we take a stride, but when we run with a few friends, we find ourselves going six miles. Groups can make us stronger.

ELEVATING OTHERS ON THE TEAM

In order for leaders to help build collective leader efficacy within their ILT, they must elevate the voices and contributions of the individuals on the team; this has often been referred to as *distributed leadership*. When it comes to distributed leadership, Viviane Robinson (2008) says there is

> [an] assumption that under a pattern of distributed leadership more of the expertise and talent of staff will be identified, developed, and utilized than under a more traditional hierarchical pattern. This argument seems particularly compelling given the breadth and depth of pedagogical expertise required to meet today's ambitious goal of all students succeeding on intellectually challenging curricula. (p. 242)

Working in a collective, such as that of an ILT, means that leadership will need to be distributed, with individual tasks assigned to different people on the team. Robinson (2008, p. 244) identified five tasks that leaders, and therefore ILTs, should focus on. Those five tasks are written here, followed by their effect size. An effect size of .40 equates to a year's worth of growth for a year's worth of input.

TASKS THAT LEADERS SHOULD FOCUS ON

1. Establishing goals (.42)

2. Strategic resourcing (.31)

3. Establishing an orderly and supportive environment (.27)

4. Planning, coordinating, and evaluating teaching and the curriculum (.42)

5. Promoting and participating in teacher learning and development (.84)

Many of you may look at strategic resourcing and establishing an orderly and safe environment and notice that they have less than a .40 effect size. You may wonder, why bother with tasks that have a low effect size? I don't subscribe to the notion that an influence under .40 is not worth doing. I believe that there is a time and place when those influences may indeed be effective. Establishing an orderly and safe environment and being strategic about our resources helps foster the ability to do the other three tasks on the list. Even though establishing an orderly and safe environment has an effect size below .40, it's hard to challenge the importance of doing that work. In fact, during COVID, the task that received the most reaction from participants in remote workshops I facilitated was establishing an orderly and supportive environment. During a pandemic, people highly disputed the low effect size of this task. A low effect size doesn't mean we ignore a task. Rather, we must understand how to put it into practice so that it will be more impactful.

Promoting and participating in teacher learning and development is most impactful when it comes to student learning. We will discuss that more in Chapter 6, which will focus on the driver of professional learning and development. Strategic resourcing is how you decide to spend your money and time. Planning, coordinating, and evaluating teaching—as well as establishing goals—have the same effect size and impact. We will explore those much deeper in Section III of this book.

Robinson says that a leader may influence others through "force, coercion, and manipulation" (2008, p. 247). Understandably, this is not the best way to lead and certainly doesn't help build a collaborative ILT.

Robinson suggests three ways to approach distributed leadership processes with a focus on student outcomes, which coincides well with a focus on learning. Following each of Robinson's three suggestions (in italics) are my additional comments:

1. *Track those influence attempts that cause changes in the thoughts and/or actions of followers.* This means paying attention to what actions are helping members of the team evolve in their thinking.

2. *Distinguish those attempts that are based on those influence processes associated with leadership rather than with manipulation, coercion, or force.* How are the actions of the team improving because of intrinsically motivated growth—and not because they are being manipulated to make the improvements?

3. *Track the impact of the change in followers for student outcomes.* What evidence is the ILT collecting to understand their growth and impact? The followers that Robinson is referring to here are those teachers engaged in the work.

Building collective leader efficacy is about understanding one another, truly collaborating, and understanding impact. It doesn't merely look good from the outside looking in; it is valued within the group as well and is not seen as contrived. Hargreaves and Fullan (2012) say that collaboration is too often seen as contrived congeniality; it becomes about the leader's vision and not about the collective thoughts of the group. Hargreaves et al. write, "Worst of all, when teachers conform to the principal's vision, this takes away the opportunity for the principal's own learning—for the development of his or her own professional capital" (p. 168). As you can see from Figure 1.1 below, when it comes to the ILT, the building leader is part of the group and not the dominant member of the group.

Leithwood and Jantzi (2008) found that

> school leaders' collective efficacy was an important link between district conditions and both the conditions found in schools and their effects on student achievement. School leaders' sense of collective efficacy also had a strong, positive relationship with leadership practices found to be effective in earlier studies. (p. 496)

There is never a better time to focus on our collective impact than now. Harris (2013, p. 551) writes, "To build the leadership capacity within their school, formal leaders need to harness the collective will,

Figure 1.1 Instructional Leadership Team: No Hierarchy

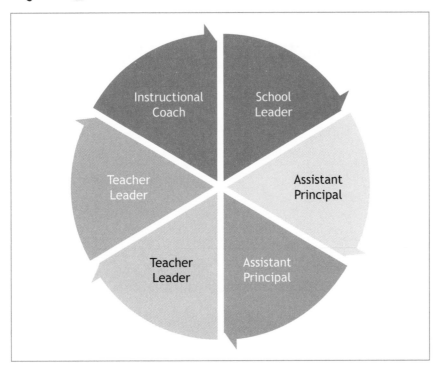

skill, and leadership of all those in their organisation in a carefully sequenced way so that the organisation, as a whole, benefits."

When leaders enter into a collaborative space, the atmosphere of those meetings can take on a different tone. As a leadership coach, I have attended many leadership meetings in which assistant principals did not speak until the leader spoke first. I have actually attended meetings in which a school leader spouted off everything they were doing to address the concerns we talked about as a group, then the leader left to take a phone call and an assistant principal spoke up and said they were not doing anything the principal had mentioned. That type of dynamic chips away at the credibility of the team.

With ILTs, we have to acknowledge that hierarchical positions exist within the school, but within the group, we need to find ways to equalize the status of school building leaders with that of the individuals around the table in order for the group to effectively do their work. To maximize our opportunity to build collective leader efficacy, we have to shift our mindsets about what the group may look like and how it may function. We have to decide who is on the team, and what role they play in the collective.

NOTES

Take a moment to consider all that you have read.

WHAT ROLES ARE INCLUDED ON THE LEADERSHIP TEAM?

The collective leader efficacy process has the potential to significantly influence the behavior of others and our own behavior, too, but only if our teams are comprised of the right people and they understand what role they play on the team. In many schools, an ILT is comprised of the school building leader, assistant principal, teachers, department chairs, instructional coaches, and paraprofessionals who can represent the voices of teacher aides. Is it possible or plausible for you to include students on the ILT or consider how a student council can assist in the work of your ILT?

Pont et al. (2008) found that "instructional leadership teams, rather than just one person, play a vital role in school development" (p. 73). There are times when ILTs are comprised of building leaders and their assistant principals, but the issue with this small group dynamic is that teachers do not feel represented, and therefore, the teams will ultimately run into issues of teachers and staff feeling as if they do not have a voice. Keep in mind that getting people to want to be on the team is not always easy, especially if they feel as though the team is all show and no go.

As a former school principal, grade-level representatives chose to be on the ILT based on their annual professional performance review (APPR), which ultimately meant that one of the yearly goals they chose was to be part of a stakeholder group. As for the paraprofessionals on the team, the same reasoning went into their decision to be on the team. Every year, teachers and paraprofessionals had to choose a goal for the given year, and the paraprofessionals who joined the team used the experience to meet their yearly goal requirement. If we look at the yearly goal as one of growth, then the ILT could be a perfect method to drive that growth. Collective leader efficacy is not about echo chambers comprised of members who simply agree with the school leader, because in order to get to the deep work, there needs to be an authentic representation of the school community. An application process (see Appendix 1) can help identify ideal candidates. Consider what roles are needed on the team. Begin thinking about the various roles that can make up the collective.

INSTRUCTIONAL LEADERSHIP TEAM ROLES

As a collective, decide on the following: What roles do we need on our team? Who should take on each role? Should roles rotate throughout the year?

- **Co-chairs:** Two people in charge of managing the instructional leadership meeting. The co-chairs set the agenda with input from other team members. I suggest that the school building leader not be one of the co-chairs in order to elevate the voices and contributions of teachers.

- **Facilitator of learning:** This position should rotate to a different person for each meeting. They may facilitate a learning activity at the ILT meeting or they may be the one designated to lead learning at a particular faculty meeting.

(Continued)

(Continued)

- **Visual representation:** One or more people who sketch during the meeting to provide a visual representation of the thoughts and actions that occurred. These visuals will be powerful representations of the work of the group. Sketching supplements notetaking because it offers another layer of understanding.

- **Researcher:** One or more people who take on the role of researching student engagement, instructional strategies, or some other aspect of the instructional core goal. This research will help the team understand how different strategies are supposed to look or when it is best to use them.

- **Notetaker:** Someone who records who said what at what time and who is responsible for completing each action step decided on by the team.

- **Critical friends:** These members provide important understandings of why some in the school community may not want to focus on a particular goal. Critical friends can also offer a historical perspective on whether past school teams have tried the same goal and why those teams may have failed.

- **Innovator:** This person doesn't only see what is, they see all of the possibilities of what could be. (Thank you to my friends from New Brunswick Teacher's Association in Canada for this one.)

- **Student members:** If possible, invite two students to be on the ILT.

IN THE END

Our teams are constantly at risk of breaking down due to the enormous challenges that they face. When I was a school principal, my team picked me up when I was down and I did the same for them. We learned from one another and listened to what each had to say. We did not always feel our voices mattered at the state or national level, but we did feel that our voices mattered within the building.

To recap, collective groups should

- create opportunities for reciprocal learning with one another,

- develop each other's leadership mindset,

- understand the necessity for a sense of well-being,

- develop each other's skill and confidence to work together as a collective, and

- develop strategies to create a positive impact on the school community.

Only then can you move forward and focus on improvement. We know that leaders cannot do this work alone. Costanza et al. (1987, p. 79) wrote, "While principals must set the organizational tone and climate, they have neither the time nor, in many cases, the subject-specific expertise to direct and influence all aspects of the instructional program."

I want our teams to be more human. There is so much divisiveness in the world; our leadership teams should be a place where we can come together and work out some of our greatest issues in a more human way. It's something we want our students to do, so we should learn to do it as well. To do this, members of the ILT need to develop both a learner's mindset so they can enter into classrooms and school-based decisions with curiosity and a leadership mindset so they can step up and lead through the learning they do. That is the focus of Chapter 2.

GUIDING QUESTIONS

- What is social cognitive theory and why does it matter to the work we do in schools?

- Why does someone who has self-efficacy in one situation not have it in another?

- How does the research focusing on self-efficacy explain some of the difficult situations we find ourselves in as leaders?

- What is leadership efficacy and why does it explain the reason that some leaders so easily take on what others see as controversial issues?

- How might student councils be inspired by the work around self and collective efficacy?

- What is the cycle that needs to take place in order for collective teacher efficacy to be built?

- What is collective leader efficacy and why should it be a driver for school improvement?

(Continued)

(Continued)

What are two questions you wish I had asked?

1.

2.

What are three areas of new learning you experienced while reading this chapter?

1.

2.

3.

NOTES

DRIVERS NECESSARY TO DEVELOP COLLECTIVE LEADER EFFICACY

DEVELOPING A LEADER AND LEARNER MINDSET

2

When we expect certain behaviors of others, we are likely to act in ways that make the expected behavior more likely to occur.

Robert Rosenthal and Elisha Babad (1985, p. 36)

THEORY OF ACTION

If . . . individuals on a team develop mindsets that focus on learning, leading, and collaboration then . . . the instructional leadership team will be able to engage in deeper and more challenging conversations around learning.

GUIDING QUESTIONS

- Has your leadership team considered drivers to developing your instructional leadership team?

- Does your school have a common understanding of what *mindset* means? Does it match Carol Dweck's definition?

- What is Stephen Rhinesmith's definition of mindset? Which experiences have most shaped your mindset?

- Why is mindset an important driver to building collective leader efficacy?

- How are you hoping your mindset will change while working with your instructional leadership team?

DRIVERS FOR SUCCESSFUL LEADERSHIP TEAMS

What contributes to our individual or team success? Are there necessary components or ingredients for the recipe to make a functional and impactful team? Just like for any athlete, musician, or actor, there are strategies that help contribute to their success. When those contributions are fostered and practiced consistently, we are more likely to be successful. In education, these contributions are often referred to as *drivers*.

Fullan (2011, p. 3) suggests four criteria where drivers are concerned, which he says, "All of which must be met in concert." Drivers of improvement should

1. foster intrinsic motivation of teachers and students,

2. engage educators and students in continuous improvement of instruction and learning,

3. inspire collective or team work,

4. affect all teachers and students—100 percent?

Unfortunately, too many instructional leadership teams (ILTs) do not consider the drivers needed to be successful when it comes to how their teams function. Since our childhood, collaborative efforts in school have focused on completing a project rather than on proactive strategies that help foster collaboration in the first place. An adult would typically intervene if we were not getting along, but my guess is that in most of our experiences, we did not receive guidance on how we each play a role in the process nor were we taught strategies for what to do when group work ground to a halt. When we got stuck, we were told to figure it out but were not offered an example or an understanding of how a group overcomes obstacles together.

As adults, we find ourselves on various teams. Perhaps we are asked to be on the team because we are an outstanding teacher in the classroom or because we have the type of personality a leader is looking for, which sometimes means we do not speak a lot or go against the grain. Other times, the team is forced to work together. Professional learning communities (PLCs) are a popular method of building teacher teams. However, citing a Boston Consulting Group Study (2014), Hargreaves and O'Connor (2018b) write,

> Professional learning communities (PLCs) were one of the most disliked forms of professional development among surveyed teachers, even though providers and administrators were highly supportive of the approach. (p. 21)

How does that happen? How can administrators support something that teachers clearly state they didn't like? Hargreaves and O'Connor (2018b) go on to write,

> A given PLC model may seem to offer a promising blueprint for collective inquiry and shared decision making. But if teachers see it as (just another) reform imposed on them from above, then they'll likely experience it as such. The protocols and terminology may be new, but they'll grumble about being forced, yet again, to go through the motions of meeting with each other, agreeing on group norms, defining shared goals, and so on. (p. 21)

Too often we provide different names to our collaborative groups, but if we do not go about understanding the process differently, the results will end up being the same. If we truly want to be successful in our team, we need to consider the drivers necessary to help the team be successful. Although the product that comes at the end of our collaborative time is important, equally as important is the process we engage in to get there and the learning we acquire during that time.

In Section II, we will explore eight different drivers necessary to develop a more impactful school team and build collective leader efficacy. These eight drivers are interdependent of each other and based on research. Additionally, you will also learn some examples of necessary actions needed to help develop the drivers. For a moment, I'd like you to engage in some reflection. Work with your team to briefly talk about what you believe is needed to build a successful ILT.

REFLECTION

Before you read the list of drivers, discuss with a partner or team what you all believe are three necessary drivers to a successful team. List them here:

1.

2.

3.

As you begin reading the drivers, consider where your examples fit into the ones provided for you. Although the words may be different, you may find that they are conceptually the same.

The drivers are mindset, well-being, context beliefs, working conditions, professional learning and development, organizational commitment, the skills to work in collectives, and the confidence to work in collectives. It is important to note that teams can focus on drivers before they work together or after years of working together when they need a reboot.

Context beliefs, working conditions, and organizational commitment have been well-explored in the collective efficacy research over the last couple of decades. Mindset, well-being, professional learning and development, the skills to work in collectives, and the confidence to work in collectives are new contributions that I am offering to the collective efficacy research. That was purposeful on my part because I believe they help expand on the research and are tied to the four experiences found by Bandura (1997).

For example, professional learning and development intersects with Bandura's (1997) research on vicarious experiences. According to Bandura, vicarious experiences offer an opportunity to raise one's self-efficacy or develop collective efficacy. In order to engage in a vicarious experience where one person can learn from another, there needs to be an opportunity. When ILTs can provide professional learning and development opportunities for staff to engage in deep learning and not superficial compliance activities, they can learn vicariously from one another.

This intersection between Bandura's (1997) four experiences and the necessary drivers to foster collective leader efficacy among an ILT brings us to the first driver: mindset.

When writing about mastery experiences, Bandura (1997, p. 80) says, "Enactive mastery experiences are the most influential source of efficacy information because they provide the most authentic evidence of whether one can muster whatever it takes to succeed." How do we muster whatever it takes to succeed and develop a conviction together if we do not all have the proper mindset to engage in that work? How do we take on our biggest issues of race, equity, deeper learning, and developing a more humane school climate if we lack the mindset to work collaboratively, listen, and learn from one another?

THE IMPACT OF MINDSET

When we hear the word *mindset,* our thoughts typically go to the work of Carol Dweck, a well-known researcher from Stanford University. Dweck wrote *Mindset: The New Psychology of Success* in 2006. Dweck's work focuses on whether students see their intelligence as fixed, meaning something they cannot change, or whether students see their intelligence as something that can develop over time by putting in effort and feel confident enough to try new strategies to gain deeper learning.

Unfortunately, over the years, Dweck's mindset work has been misunderstood and misused by educators in classrooms and schools around the world—so much so that Dweck wrote a clarification of her research in *Education Week.* In the article, Dweck (2015) clarifies the difference between having a growth mindset and having a fixed mindset:

> Students who believed their intelligence could be developed (a growth mindset) outperformed those who believed their intelligence was fixed (a fixed mindset). And when students learned through a structured program that they could "grow their brains" and increase their intellectual abilities, they did better. Finally, we found that having children focus on the process that leads to learning (like hard work or trying new strategies) could foster a growth mindset and its benefits.

This is the perfect example of how beliefs and actions intersect. Students believed they could grow as learners, especially when given challenging material, and in the end, they grew as learners. Wouldn't it be great if our school leadership teams approached their work on the team in the same way? Wouldn't it be more powerful if people went to team meetings with the mindset to learn together through a process? Shouldn't our ILTs foster curiosity among adults as much as those adults try to foster curiosity among students? Unfortunately, it was not that clear for everyone. Dweck (2015) went on to write about the often-misunderstood aspect of the growth mindset research:

> A growth mindset isn't just about effort. Perhaps the most common misconception is simply equating the growth mindset with effort. Certainly, effort is key for students' achievement, but it's not the only thing. Students need to try new strategies and seek input from others when they're stuck. They need this repertoire of approaches— not just sheer effort—to learn and improve.

Trying new strategies and seeking the help of others is not only important for students; it has implications for adults as well. The research on efficacy clearly shows there are areas where people feel efficacious and areas where they do not. As you read through this book, you will learn that seeking the help of others is key when it comes to building collective efficacy. A fixed mindset is characterized by not seeking out feedback and not trying to learn. Having a fixed mindset can lead us to hold deficit mindsets in which we believe that some students are capable of excelling while we do not believe that other students are capable of the same growth.

STUDENT COUNCIL REFLECTION

How can mindset research impact how students work together on a student council? Consider introducing the student council to articles or developmentally appropriate videos focusing on growth mindset research.

A DEFICIT MINDSET

Some adults in school hold deficit mindsets regarding students who are Black, brown, Latinx, or English language learners or students from indigenous backgrounds such as First Nations communities, Maori students in New Zealand, and Aboriginal students in Australia. Davis and Museus (2019) write, "Deficit thinking is rooted in *a blame the victim* orientation that suggests that people are responsible for their predicament and fails to acknowledge that they live within coercive systems that cause harm with no accountability."

The authors go on to write, "Deficit thinking is not only a symptom of larger systemic oppression, but also reinforces these oppressive systems. Furthermore, deficit thinking is pervasive and implicit, and often emerging in language that treats people as problems" (Davis & Museus, 2019). Perry (2020, p. 38) writes, "The deficit perspective—the conscious or unconscious belief that members of a disenfranchised cultural group don't have the skills to achieve because of their cultural background."

To provide an example of what this looks like, Boser et al. (2014) writes,

> Secondary teachers predicted that high-poverty students were 53 percent less likely to earn a college diploma than their more affluent peers. They also believed that African American students were 47 percent less likely to graduate from college than their white peers. Finally, they believed that Hispanic students were 42 percent less likely to earn a college diploma than their white peers.

Deficit thinking intertwines with that of the Pygmalion effect, which can be explained: "When we expect certain behaviors of others, we are likely to act in ways that make the expected behavior more likely to occur" (Rosenthal & Babad, 1985, p. 36). Rosenthal and Jacobson (1968, p. 20) found that "one person's expectations of another's behavior may come to serve as a self-fulfilling prophecy. When teachers expected that certain children would show greater intellectual development, those children did show greater intellectual development."

As a school community, deficit thinking isn't only dangerous for marginalized students; it is also dangerous for how members of the ILT view their colleagues. In my practice, I try to take a nonjudgmental approach to teachers and leaders I work with. Can you say the same? Do you have certain colleagues whom you view through a deficit lens? How can you change your mindset to give them a fair shot as opposed to setting up a self-fulfilling prophecy?

Take a moment with your team to consider the following questions and reflect on what they might mean for your school.

REFLECT

Have you considered deficit thinking before?

How has it impacted you?

Do you have colleagues who you view through a deficit lens?

How will you suspend those feelings and change your language to give them a fair shot?

 **NOTES**

This discussion is important because, as a member of the ILT, you may be asked to do learning walks in a variety of different types of classrooms or run an activity during professional learning and development. To do that fairly, you must have a learner's mindset. Figure 2.1 Change Your Mindset is focused on how you can change your mindset toward ideas or colleagues within your school.

Figure 2.1 Change Your Mindset

Instead of . . .	Try to . . .
Focusing on change	Focus on improvement
Walking into an instructional leadership team meeting with one idea and wanting to walk out with the same idea	Walk into an instructional leadership team meeting with one idea and walk out with a better idea due to the collective thoughts of others
Feeling improvement in your gut	Collect evidence to understand impact
Seeing debate as a negative interaction	See debate as an opportunity for growth
Staying in your comfort zone	Engage in a new challenge
Deferring to the group	Engage in collective responsibility
Seeing a colleague as resistant	Understand that your colleague may lack self-efficacy in that area
Create some of your own examples:	

Source: DeWitt, 2021.

CHALLENGES CAN HELP SHIFT OUR MINDSET

Rhinesmith (1992) defines *mindset* as "a predisposition to see the world in a particular way . . . a filter through which we look at the world" (p. 63) and expanded the definition in 1995 by saying it "is a way of being rather than a set of skills. It is an orientation of the world that allows one to see certain things that others do not" (p. 276). As described earlier, we have to understand that biases can impact how we see the world, and those biases can contribute to our mindsets. Having a growth mindset and an ability to recognize our biases is an important step to opening up how we view the world.

In 2020 and 2021, our experience of COVID-19 impacted our mindsets greatly in a variety of ways. Prior to COVID, I was on the road running in-person workshops. Once COVID became a pandemic, all of that changed. The sessions were canceled, rescheduled, or went to remote learning sessions. I was coaching middle school and high school leadership teams, in California, and their schools were not back in person until the late spring of 2021. Every month over those 14 months, we had scheduled 90-minute sessions. Those 90-minute sessions needed to be impactful because school leaders were stressed and many were concerned that they were not doing enough for their teachers and students.

We decided that remote walk-throughs would be the best method to understanding what remote teaching looked like. We developed the remote walk-through process together and learned from each other as we went through it. Our shift in mindset created a great learning experience for all of us and helped us all understand, perhaps in small ways, what teachers and students were experiencing when it came to remote learning. The following blog explains how we entered into the process with a growth mindset.

How Team Walk-Throughs Can Engage Educators in Remote Learning

by Peter DeWitt

First published on October 4, 2020, in
Finding Common Ground on EdWeek.org

As we all get a little bit more used to remote learning, for those of us not able to be back fully in person yet, on one of the most memorable World Teachers Days we will ever witness, one of the ways we can start to improve our practices as leaders and teachers is through the walk-through process. A recent team experience really opened up the possibility of team walk-throughs, which can help build a common language and a common understanding around what learning could look like in a remote or hybrid classroom. (It definitely works for in-person situations, too, but it can be a bit intimidating. I'll get to that later.)

First and foremost, it's important to say that many teachers around the world still involved in a remote or hybrid experience are doing an extraordinary amount of work preparing for the learning that takes place in the classroom. World Teachers Day is not just

---

about celebrating teachers, it is also about focusing on how they impact learning. They not only have to plan for synchronous and asynchronous lessons, but they also have to deal with the fact that some students are not showing up because they are still essential workers in their own families and some students are showing up, but they are ghosting the teacher.

What's Ghosting?

In working with a middle school group of leaders, their teachers began to figure out that some students were signing into their Google classroom account to get the credit, but because they were allowed to keep their screens off (i.e., privacy, bandwidth, etc.), they were leaving the actual room to watch television or play games on their handheld devices. They were not paying attention to the teacher teaching the lesson. Some of the ghosting issues were dealt with by allowing students to keep their screens on, texting parents to make sure that they knew their children were ghosting the teacher, or using Go Guardian so teachers could see that their students were following along on their district-sponsored laptop.

What's important to remember before we dive into the team walk-through process is that whether we find ourselves in a remote or hybrid situation, the reality is that recent research shows that there is a concern about temporary learning loss and long-term disengagement from school. Teachers and leaders in schools talk often about the concern of learning loss as well. This issue of ghosting certainly contributes to the concern of learning loss and disengagement.

What that means is, regardless of how hard it is to find ways to engage students in learning, we need to keep the energy going. Part of how we do that is to encourage team walk-throughs so different stakeholders in a school can discuss what seems to be working with students in some classrooms and learn from one another when it comes to student engagement and instructional strategies, which can ultimately build collective efficacy in a school.

The Process

A few weeks ago, I worked with groups of middle and high school principals, who I have been working with monthly over several years. Over two days, nine teams of school leaders (principal, assistant principals) ranging from two to five people, were engaged in 90-minute coaching sessions. In our in-person sessions pre-COVID, many of us had engaged in team walk-throughs.

Teachers voluntarily allowed us to come into their classroom for 10 minutes at a time so we could calibrate what we see and develop a common language and common understanding together. The challenge

(Continued)

(Continued)

was to engage in those same conversations from my home office in upstate New York and the main offices of the leadership teams in schools in central California.

In the first session, it was suggested that the principal share their screen and enter into each teacher's classroom remotely. Those of us working with the principal muted our screens to make sure that our voices would not be heard in the teacher's session through the principal's computer.

One of the instant changes I noticed from our in-person walk-throughs is that it was less intimidating to the teacher. Why? The teacher and students only saw the principal enter the remote classroom, which they were already used to, and they did not see the other two to five of us who were seeing their class through the shared screen.

Over the hours I was engaged in the practice of team walk-throughs with different leadership teams, I felt the process evolve. For example, I found we needed to keep the chat box open in the teacher's classroom so we could see the students interacting with the teacher through our shared principal screen. Remember that when we enter into virtual classes, we often have to open the chat box because it does not automatically open for us. The chat box in the teacher's classroom gives us a lot of information when it comes to student engagement and student dialogue.

In one of the 90-minute sessions, I was working with a principal and four assistant principals who lead a 3,000-student high school. The team has a lot of comradery, and I have had the good fortune to get to know them over three years. In the team walk-through sessions with them, we not only shared the screen of the principal, which allowed us a window into the remote teaching classrooms, the principal also made sure the chat box was open and observable in each classroom, and we used our shared chat box as an admin team to discuss what we were seeing. It was a powerful way to spend 90 minutes, and the admin team decided it was something they would continue to do even when I am not present.

The last 90-minute team walk-through session was a little different but equally as powerful. The principal of that high school had been working on a collaborative walk-through document with his teachers, so as our admin team began the team walk-throughs, he tried out the new walk-through document to see if it provided the impact he and his teachers were hoping for. He found that he needed to tweak certain sections, but overall, it was going to prove to be an impactful tool to use with teachers.

As a school principal, I often walked into a meeting and walked out with a better one because I was open to the feedback of the teachers in the building I led. I approach coaching in the same way. I find that we have agreed-upon topics we need to discuss, but how we go about the process is best left up to our group.

What we know is that we are all worried about learning loss, but doing nothing about it won't change that end result. Remote walk-throughs are one way that leaders can develop a common language and common understanding, get an idea of the successes and challenges of remote and hybrid teaching, and decide on next steps with their teachers. Walk-throughs should not be about judgment, but instead, they should be about learning from one another.

The collaboration between all of us led to the idea of using one screen as opposed to all of us individually entering into a remote classroom, which is intimidating and not very collaborative. It also led us to studying the chat box and looking to see how teachers use it in the classroom. We were able to discuss what I believe are the most important elements of a classroom experience (in person, remote, hybrid), which are the use of learning intentions, success criteria, teacher clarity, a classroom discussion strategy, and examples of synchronous and asynchronous learning.

This COVID educational experience is hard enough that sometimes we have to look at the positives, and it was truly inspiring to watch teachers engage students as we engage in deeper conversations as an administration team.

Thanks to the admin teams. You know who you are!

Having a learner's mindset can help us become much more innovative. A learner's mindset helped me take what I had learned from in-person walk-throughs and transfer over that learning to remote walk-throughs, collaboratively working with the leadership teams to create an even more impactful process. That learning transferred to the webinars and remote workshops I was facilitating because seeing what teachers and students were experiencing in the classroom provided me with an understanding of what I needed to focus on when it came to learning during webinars and remote workshops. When we bring together mindset, especially one that involves growth, and then match it up to skills and practices, we can develop effective methods to engage in dialogue around learning, regardless of our challenges.

FOSTERING LEADERSHIP ON YOUR TEAM

When we think of topics that rock our instruction core—such as racism, gender discrimination, white privilege, and deficit mindset, among others—we know that we need groups of educators within a building that have the moral compass and courage to take on these issues to develop a better school climate for students and adults. We know that this courage takes development because leading through these conversations can be scary.

> We need groups of educators within a building that have the moral compass and courage to take on these issues to develop a better school climate for students and adults.

Kennedy et al. (2013, p. 10) write, "Leadership development is less directly concerned with developing a set of discrete skills and is increasingly concerned with participants' underlying assumptions and how these shape possibilities for the future." Hence, this refers to the need for a more robust discussion around mindset and the other drivers you will learn about in this book.

Underlying assumptions need to be addressed through conversations and deep work if teams are to foster the mindsets of individuals on the team and in the school community. Leadership, teaching, and learning are ever evolving because of the complex issues we face in schools, and we need to be prepared to evolve with it. Kennedy et al. (2013, p. 12) write, "Conceptualizations of leadership are shifting and this in turn influences where we look for it." Where we need to look for it is within our ILT, among the assistant principals, teacher leaders, and instructional coaches around the table.

Costanza et al. (1987, p. 82) found the following:

1. A school district may symbolically and substantively establish improved instruction as a goal by focusing energy and resources on developing departmental leadership.

2. Department coordinators and administrators working together as a group with a common purpose will develop normative values that will significantly affect formal and informal communication channels.

3. An infrastructure of department coordinators within the schools will influence the focus of activities and nudge more instructional issues onto department and building agendas.

4. Shared decision making and involvement with the meaningful work of instruction have a positive impact on teachers' attitudes and sense of commitment.

This driver of developing a learner's mindset (as well as one that focuses on leadership) is a good start in the process of supporting the research of Costanza, but the forthcoming drivers will help teams reach deeper into that process. Before we end the focus on mindset, let's cover some possible action steps.

It's easy to talk about the need for a developed mindset but it's a lot harder to help foster it. Using Bandura's four experiences that foster efficacy among individuals and teams, I have provided some examples of how to focus on mindset among the ILT.

WHERE SOURCES OF EFFICACY INTERSECT WITH MINDSET

Mastery Experiences

➤ **See challenges as opportunities.** Some of our best learning opportunities are masked as challenges. If we sit around wringing our hands because things are hard, we will never truly understand that those challenges offer us an opportunity to work together as a team and learn about our colleagues and ourselves.

- **Flipped faculty meetings.** When I was a school principal, it was during a time of great accountability; teachers in my building said they felt like they lacked a voice in their own learning. We worked together to flip faculty meetings so we could focus on learning.

- **Cultural responsiveness.** It was during a conversation with Zaretta Hammond on A Seat at the Table (*Education Week*) that I realized that although I had a strong focus on equity, I still had a very specific perspective that needed to be opened and expanded upon.

- **Crisis can be a teacher.** It is through crisis that we can learn some of our greatest lessons. Challenging times offer us mastery experiences.

(Continued)

(Continued)

> **Cycles of inquiry.** In Section III, your team will learn about using a cycle of inquiry to focus improvement efforts in your school community. Some steps in the cycle will not be easy, but during those challenging times, your team will find great opportunities to grow.

- **Vicarious Experiences**

  > **Model the mindset.** As school building leaders (everyone on the leadership team), we can model the mindset we want to see by taking risks and trying new strategies. Whether it's when leaders take a risk and focus on an instructional strategy that teachers can then use in their classrooms or engaging in dialogue with all staff about topics of race, gender, and equity, we can model a learner's mindset and a leader's mindset every day in our schools if we make the effort to do so.

  > **Common language/common understanding.** To develop mindsets, we must engage in activities that will build a common language and understanding around the words we use in our schools. Appendix 2 has a sticky note activity that can be used in an ILT meeting to begin building an understanding of certain concepts and cultivating mindsets of collaboration.

- **Social Persuasion**

  > **Decision-making.** Increase the decision-making power of teachers within the building so they understand that their voices matter. When teachers have decision-making power on an ILT, it builds both independence and interdependence.

  > **DEI model.** Develop a DEI model within your ILT:

    - **Diversity.** Make sure that your ILT includes a range of thinkers (included in this book is an application process to be a member of the team). We always need a mix of rule followers and instigators on our team.

    - **Equity.** Although we will get into this deeper when exploring the skills to work in collectives, it's important that we engage in communication strategies that allow equity of voice. No one person should dominate the conversation.

- **Inclusion.** Diversity and equity lead to inclusion when people on the team understand their voices matter, even if that means hearing them when they disagree with us.

- Affective States

  - **Collaboration.** Foster a school climate that focuses on working together, not one where teachers feel they need to compete for the attention of school building leaders. This will increase their excitement to be in the group.

  - **Short Surveys.** Engage members of the ILT in short surveys during the inquiry process (Section III) to gain an understanding of what is working and what is not. Use the results to improve the process, and be open about how the surveys helped improve the process so that the members of the team understand that their voices matter. This feedback survey process will increase the affective state of members.

IN THE END

Understanding mindset is important when it comes to how individuals on the ILT interact with one another. It's also important to shift your mindset when you are confronted with challenges. As school building leaders and teacher leaders, you have the opportunity to impact the mindsets of your colleagues—but only if you can shift the conversation and be the model for the change needed.

Many times, teacher leaders struggle with how they see themselves, and they may look to the skillsets of other leaders and try to match up with those skills that everyone believes leaders need to possess. Skills are definitely important, but the mindset of growth is equally as important. Leadership is not something you either have or you don't. Leadership can be developed, and it's important that every single member of the ILT can see themselves stepping up to take on leadership roles. The collective team is not about individuals being passive; instead, those collective teams should be focused on how they inspire growth in each other.

GUIDING QUESTIONS

- Has your leadership team considered drivers to developing your instructional leadership team?

- Does your school have a common understanding of what *mindset* means? Does it match Carol Dweck's definition?

- What is Stephen Rhinesmith's definition of mindset? Which experiences have most shaped your mindset?

- Why is mindset an important driver to building collective leader efficacy?

- How are you hoping your mindset will change while working with your instructional leadership team?

What two questions do you wish I had asked?

1.

2.

What three new areas of learning did you experience while reading this chapter?

1.

2.

3.

NOTES

MENTAL HEALTH AND WELL-BEING

Emotions are the most powerful force inside the workplace—as they are in every human endeavor. They influence everything from leadership effectiveness to building and maintaining complex relationships, from innovation to customer relations.

Marc Brackett (2019, p. 222)

THEORY OF ACTION

If . . . teams can focus on mental health and well-being, then . . . they will work together to take actionable steps to lower their stress and will develop more proactive strategies to confront their challenges.

GUIDING QUESTIONS

- Why is mental health and well-being an area where we need to take action?
- In what ways can we focus on mental health and well-being both personally and professionally?
- How does your school community address the needs of adult mental health?
- When it comes to well-being, what are your next steps?

THE STATISTICS ON LEADERS' WELL-BEING

In the United States, 42% of principals indicated they were considering leaving their position (Levin et al., 2020). According to the Learning Policy Institute,

> Nationally, the average tenure of a principal is about four years, and nearly one in five principals, approximately 18 percent, turn over annually. Often the schools that need the most capable principals, those serving students from low-income families, have even greater principal turnover. (Levin et al., 2020, p. 3)

The Australian Principal Occupational Health, Safety and Wellbeing Survey shows that "1 in 3 school principals are in serious distress and 1 in 3 principals have actually been exposed to physical violence" (Riley et al., 2019, p. 177). The Center for Creative Leadership found that

> eighty-eight percent of leaders report that work is a primary source of stress in their lives and that having a leadership role increases the level of stress. More than 60 percent of surveyed leaders cite their organizations as failing to provide them with the tools they need to manage stress. (Campbell et al., 2017, p. 3)

Queen and Schumacher (*Principal Magazine*) found that "as many as 75 percent of principals experience stress-related symptoms that include fatigue, weakness, lack of energy, irritability, heartburn, headache, trouble sleeping, sexual dysfunction, and depression" (2006, p. 18). Additionally, Van der Merwe et al. (2011) found that "school principals experience high levels of stress that hamper their self-efficacy and inhibit their executive control capacities" (p. 666). All of the above statistics were from pre-COVID times.

When it came to COVID, we learned that stress and anxiety were palpable. During the COVID pandemic, a Yale Center for Emotional Intelligence study of over 1,000 school leaders in New York City described it in this way:

> Leaders were asked to share the three emotions they had experienced the most during the prior two weeks. An overwhelming 95 percent of the feelings they named could be classified as "negative."

> The most commonly mentioned emotion was anxiety, which stood out glaringly above all others—overwhelmed, sad, stressed, frustrated, uncertain, and worried. (Brackett et al., 2020)

When reading the survey results from the Yale Center study, it is not surprising that during the COVID pandemic, school leaders would feel a high amount of stress. However, prior to the pandemic, research showed that the job of school leaders has become increasingly stressful. A 2018 Penn State University study found that "principals experience substantial job-related stress, yet they often lack the guidance and resources necessary to develop their own social and emotional competencies (SECs) that could help them respond appropriately" (Mahfouz et al., 2019, p. 3).

MENTAL HEALTH SUPPORT FOR INSTRUCTIONAL LEADERSHIP TEAMS

In order for instructional leadership teams (ILTs) to build collective leader efficacy, mental health and well-being has to be a priority. Our mental health and well-being is impacted by two factors: the stress we feel at home/on the job and the emotions we feel when we are going through stress. Those two areas of stress and emotions have an impact on our mental health and well-being and therefore have an impact on how we function within our ILT. Let's begin with stress.

What we know is that the stress of the job is at an all-time high and that stress has a negative impact on our work lives and home lives. A Harvard Medical School study (2018) shows that "stress affects not only memory and many other brain functions, like mood and anxiety, but also promotes inflammation, which adversely affects heart health."

There is strong evidence that chronic stress can rewire our brains (Harvard Medical School, 2018). We know this about students who experience traumatic events, but leaders and their staff often don't consider how the effects of trauma affect their own lives. The Harvard Medical School study states, "It's much like what would happen if you exercised one part of your body and not another. The part that was activated more often would become stronger, and the part that got less attention would get weaker." The study goes on to say, "This is what appears to happen in the brain when it is under continuous stress: It essentially builds up the part of the brain designed to handle threats, and the part of the brain tasked with more complex thought takes a back seat." Stress can have a negative impact on our emotions both at home and at school. What this tells us is that the chronic stress we experience as school leaders can directly impede our ability to think creatively, solve problems, and engage in the complex work of supporting our students.

In *Permission to Feel*, Brackett (2019, pp. 219-220) writes, "Emotions are the most powerful force inside the workplace—as they are in every human endeavor. They influence everything from leadership effectiveness to building and maintaining complex relationships, from innovation to customer relations." That alone shows the reason why well-being is a driver to building collective leader efficacy.

Additionally, Brackett (2019) researched five areas that impact how we function. Those five areas are our emotional state, decision-making, social relations, physical health, and creativity and effectiveness. Brackett writes, "Our emotional state determines where we direct our attention, what we remember, and what we learn" (p. 27). That will impact our decision-making because

> when we are in the grip of a strong emotion—such as anger or sadness, but also elation and joy—we perceive the world differently and the choices we make at that moment are influenced. Being in the grip of strong emotions has the potential to impact our social relations, because it impacts how we interpret other people's feelings. (p. 27)

We know from earlier in the chapter how stress impacts our own physical health, which is the fourth area on Brackett's list. The fifth area is our creativity and effectiveness. When we are stressed and our negative emotions get the best of us, it can negatively impact our creativity, which means that we will not be as innovative as our potential allows. This is one of the main reasons that well-being needs to be a driver in developing collective leader efficacy. It is time that we begin engaging in discussions and actionable steps when it comes to the well-being of our students, teachers, and leaders. If we do not take a stronger stance on these issues, we will see more and more teachers and leaders leaving our profession.

The question now becomes, what do we do about it? That question is an important one because it means that not only do we need to talk about it within our teams and in our school communities, but we also have to do something about it—and that is not always easy.

STUDENT COUNCIL REFLECTION

We know that stress and anxiety are as much of an issue for students as for adults. How might this work look at the student council level? How could student councils make well-being a priority for their school community? Is it through literature or informational videos they send out to students or information tables they set up at school?

From a personal perspective, we can do a lot to help address our mental health and well-being. It comes down to practicing self-care and community care. The following are some of the ways we can focus on mental health and well-being that can be fostered and focused on in our personal lives and through ILT discussions.

STRATEGIES FOR IMPROVING OUR OWN MENTAL HEALTH

- **Counseling.** Seek help from a professional. Find a good match: someone who fits your style of listening and offers suggestions for improvement. Counseling can help us understand whether we are stressed or depressed. There is a difference between stress and depression, one of the biggest being that depression can sometimes lead to self-harm. The Mayo Clinic (2020) defines depression as "a mood disorder that causes a persistent feeling of sadness and loss of interest." The Mayo Clinic goes on to say, "It affects how you feel, think and behave and can lead to a variety of emotional and physical problems. You may have trouble doing normal day-to-day activities, and sometimes you may feel as if life isn't worth living. . . . More than just a bout of the blues, depression isn't a weakness, and you can't simply 'snap out' of it. Depression may require long-term treatment."

(Continued)

(Continued)

- **Mindfulness and meditation.** This is a very personal example because I deal with anxiety. I have found that meditation is a way to calm my thoughts. What began as 10 minutes a day of practice transferred into other parts of my day that I found stressful, which is where mindfulness comes into the equation. Activity 3.1 helps you understand the difference between meditation and mindfulness and put both into practice. It has encouraged me to be much more proactive than reactive in how I deal with everyday situations, even the most stressful ones. There is a great deal of research showing the benefits of meditation and mindfulness.

Activity 3.1 Meditation and Mindfulness

Meditation	Mindfulness
• Find a quiet spot. Focus on breathing for 5 to 10 minutes. • When thoughts of work arise, let them come, and then gently send them out with exhales. The point is not to push out thoughts. The point is to take a few moments to focus only on breathing and letting go of the thoughts that do come.	• Take those moments of meditation and let them inhabit as many parts of your day as possible. • When a stressful situation happens, do not forget to take a step back and breathe. • Practice slowing down by being conscious of how quickly you eat or how deeply you listen to others. • Mindfulness is about acknowledging distracting thoughts and then letting them go to be able to focus on the task at hand.

- **Social media boundaries.** Colleagues I have found through social media platforms such as Twitter and Facebook have become friends and confidants. What we have also noticed is that social media doesn't come with boundaries. It's easy to get notifications on our phones and find ourselves engaged in debates we never saw coming. Try to set your phone down in another room, turn it off, or maybe even take certain apps off your phone. I've taken Twitter and Facebook off mine and it made a world of difference.

- **Friends and family.** Plan dinners with friends or family. It's a bonus when our friends and family are not in education, which forces us to have conversations outside of our profession.

- **Exercise.** The benefits of exercise are well-known. Walk, run/jog, or ride your bike. Get outside and breathe.

- **Pleasure reading.** Pick up a noneducational book (yes, I see the irony here). Set aside time to escape from work and dive into a book in your favorite genre.

- **Journaling, blogging, and writing.** Writing in a journal can be a powerful way to address anxiety because it helps you work through the feelings you are experiencing. As a writer, I find that blogging and writing chapters help me work through ideas that I can then put into action or vice versa. I engage in actionable steps with groups and then write about them to help me figure out the process.

- **Find a hobby.** Whether it's working in the garden, making pottery, or working on an old car, we need an escape from our professional lives. Engage in an activity that allows you to connect with a deeper sense of who you are as a person.

From a professional perspective, our ILTs need to practice well-being as a team and offer suggestions to the school community on how each person can practice it as well. The following are some of the ways we can focus on our well-being as professionals and as an ILT.

WHERE SOURCES OF EFFICACY INTERSECT WITH WELL-BEING

- **Mastery Experiences**

  - **De-implementation.** ILTs spend a lot of time deciding on what to implement, but what about taking the time to decide what to de-implement? According to van Bodegom-Vos et al. (2017, p. 495), de-implementation is the process of "abandoning existing low value practices." We will focus on de-implementation in Section III when we engage in cycles of inquiry.

  - **Coaching/mentoring models.** More holistic leadership coaching in which individuals and ILTs work with a mentor or coach can be helpful for the driver of mental health and mindfulness. Leadership coaches with a social-emotional and academic component can help individuals and teams minimize stress and anxiety.

  - **Clear goals.** In their surveys of school leaders in New York City, Yale researchers found that clear goals and expectations on the part of district office leaders (where they establish consistent communication) can be a highly effective way to help minimize stress and anxiety among individuals and members of an ILT. The challenge to this strategy, and the reason why it is a mastery experience, is that consistent practice of establishing clear goals among our ILT will minimize time spent on rehashing the same topic over and over again.

- **Vicarious Experiences**

  - **Set boundaries.** Talk with teachers about setting boundaries when it comes to checking emails and giving out their cell phone numbers. I know this comes with a great deal of guilt, but boundaries are healthy. This does not mean teachers should arrive at their classroom when the students arrive and leave right after the last bell. Establishing work hours such as 7:00 AM to 3:30 PM or 8:00 AM to 4:30 PM still allows for work/life balance. Clearly, during a crisis situation, phone calls will be made and people can step up to the plate, but all teachers deserve to have down time to re-energize so they can fully be there for students during the day. As school building leaders, create an automatic email notification that says you only check email at three different times during the day (for example, 7:30 AM, 12:00 PM, and 5:00 PM). Do not check email after 5:00 PM. If there are emergencies, phone calls should be the form of communication school leaders use to notify their school communities. We need to take steps to no longer let our smartphones take over our lives.

➤ **Professional development/mindfulness training.** Penn State University researchers suggest professional development for leaders such as mindfulness interventions and emotional intelligence training. Mahfouz et al. (2019, p. 8) write, "A mindfulness-based professional development program originally designed to support teachers was recently modified to support principals. Cultivating Awareness and Resilience in Education (CARE) was designed to nurture educators' self-awareness and to help them understand and regulate their emotions with the goal of improving health and well-being. The program is based on three major instructional components: mindfulness and awareness practices (40%), emotion skills (40%), and caring and compassion skills (20%)."

Social Persuasion

➤ **Mindful interactions.** As a team of professionals, it's important to understand how we talk with one another. Dismissing an individual's opinions, abruptly shutting down conversations, or talking about people at or after meetings is never the way to create a positive team experience. Give people time to talk without interrupting them and begin each meeting by discussing the goals of the meeting so members of the team understand why they are present.

Affective States

➤ **Survey teachers.** An ILT should create a survey focusing on mental health and well-being and use the results of that survey in how they proceed as a team. Within the survey, it's not enough to ask teachers if they are feeling overwhelmed or anxious; it's also important to ask them why they feel that way. The school leadership team can use this information to look for commonalities among responses from teachers and staff and plan accordingly. This will improve the affective state of teachers and staff within the building.

➤ **Staff helpline.** Lew (2020) suggests using a staff helpline. Using a Google form, school leaders and counselors can work together to create a form that asks respondents what they need around topics such as how to teach wellness in the

(Continued)

(Continued)

classroom or what support they may need because they are feeling a great deal of anxiety within their lives. Clearly, there may be privacy concerns here, and unions would need to be involved in the process because everyone would want to make sure that there are protections in place.

▶ **Acknowledge well-being.** So many educators and leaders in a school simply ignore well-being and self-care. It's not that they do not understand that the need for it exists, but they do put it on the back burner to talk about some other time. This is not a healthy way to go through our school days.

IN THE END

In this chapter, we began by gaining an understanding of drivers. If you're fortunate enough to be developing an ILT, then you can start the team process by focusing on the drivers you will learn about throughout Section II. However, if you already have a team in place, then you can still focus on one or two drivers at a time while you do the work. For example, in working with a large urban high school in Massachusetts that already had an ILT in place, we began our work together by setting the goals for the team and defining the roles each person will play.

When it came to drivers, I worked with the team from Massachusetts on two specific drivers you will learn about at the end of Section II: the skills to work in collectives and the confidence to work in collectives. In our second meeting, we focused on well-being and professional learning and development. Start with the drivers that make sense for your team.

The driver I began with is well-being. Leaders and teachers are experiencing so much stress these days that I needed to begin with this one. The reality is that none of these personal and professional interventions will happen if we do not start making mental health and well-being more of a priority. We must not be embarrassed to talk about the mental health of leaders nor should we be ashamed to take actionable steps to help make sure that they (we) get the help they (we) need.

In my survey involving school leaders, one respondent wrote that they do not talk about stress and anxiety because they are supposed to be the role model in the school. I believe role models are the ones who talk openly about issues such as stress and anxiety and then work with staff to understand who can alleviate, or at least minimize, that stress and anxiety in school. Talking about stress and anxiety isn't a weakness, and it doesn't make us less of a role model; doing nothing and staying silent makes us less of a role model.

I once told a district, "If you want to burn your principals out, keep doing what you're doing. If you want to foster the same type of growth that we say we care about for our students, then we need to make some changes." Hargreaves et al. (2012, p. 113) write, "In collaborative cultures, failure and uncertainty are not protected and defended, but instead are shared and discussed with a view to gaining help and support."

Well-being is important to talk about because we all experienced a pandemic that increased our levels of stress. We need to focus on well-being because we know that the years leading up to the pandemic were filled with stress as well, and the last thing we should want is to continue living our work lives with so much stress. This focus on well-being leads us to our next driver, context beliefs, which we'll discuss in Chapter 4. It's easier for people to practice self-care and focus on their well-being if they believe they work in a place that will be supportive of their efforts, and that is what context beliefs are all about.

Before you move on to the next chapter, take a moment to reflect on and journal about the guiding questions. I want to make sure you leave this chapter with some actionable steps.

GUIDING QUESTIONS

- Why is mental health and well-being an area where we need to take action?
- In what ways can we focus on mental health and well-being both personally and professionally?
- How does your school community address the needs of adult mental health?
- When it comes to well-being, what are your next steps?

(Continued)

(Continued)

What two questions do you wish I had asked?

1.

2.

What three new areas of learning did you experience while reading this chapter?

1.

2.

3.

NOTES

CONTEXT BELIEFS

4

As a practical matter, on most important decisions, there is an information gap. There is usually an information gap between the solid information in hand and what is needed.

Robert Greenleaf (1977, p. 11)

THEORY OF ACTION

If . . . members of the instructional leadership team are to do their most innovative thinking, then . . . they need to feel they are within a school building or district that will support that innovative thinking.

GUIDING QUESTIONS

- What is the relationship between context beliefs and motivating individuals and a team?

- When have there been times that you felt supported to engage in innovative practices?

- When have there been times you did not feel supported to engage in innovative practices?

- When have there been times when your school building or district could say their context beliefs were not supported by you?

- In what ways can districts support the context beliefs of school leaders?

The theory of action I created for the beginning of this chapter seems like common sense. After all, of course a school building or district would want their teachers to do their most innovative thinking, right? Unfortunately, there are often school building or district initiatives that are contradictory to the innovation they say they support. What this means is that leaders within school buildings and districts may pressure teachers to follow pacing guides so much that teachers do not feel as though they can creatively teach the curriculum within those pacing guides. Or perhaps leaders within school buildings and districts say they want teachers to be innovative in their practices but do not provide teachers with adequate planning time; maybe those leaders control the agenda that teachers focus on in professional learning communities (PLCs), which gives them inadequate time to engage in creative planning for students.

How do we show teachers and leaders that we want their most innovative thinking? Is it through our words and actions? Do our actions and words actually match? Do we provide teachers and leaders with the resources they need (one of the key resources is time)? The conversation about mental health and well-being from the previous chapter and whether leaders can engage in open and honest discussions about topics such as stress and anxiety leads us to the next driver for building collective leader efficacy—context beliefs. Leithwood and Mascall (2008, p. 536) state, "These are beliefs about whether, for example, the working conditions in the school will support teachers' efforts to instruct in the manner suggested by the school's improvement initiatives." This is a double-edged sword. To explain this, I want to reuse the quotation from Dimmock (2016) that appeared in the introduction to this book:

> The level at which we think about a system is important for understanding system leadership in its contemporary context. If we take the school (meso level) as the system, then the head teacher is a system leader. However, if we consider the local authority or the nation as the system (macro level), then the head teacher of a school becomes leader of a sub-system, and to be a system leader, s(he) must contribute to the greater good of other schools beyond their own. (p. 62)

We have to understand not only the importance of leaders and teachers feeling that they work in a district that will support their efforts but also that their efforts have to contribute to the greater good. Often, as teachers and leaders, we may not feel the district we work in is supportive because we are not getting what we want, and we forget that there are times when what we want does not necessarily contribute to the greater good. There needs to be a balance here by feeling that we are supported but also understanding that support is a two-way street; we need to also be supportive of our school district. This tension is important for our students to understand as well.

STUDENT COUNCIL REFLECTION

Do students in your school feel supported? How will you help them understand that their voices matter in school decision-making? Students often feel seen and not heard. How will you help resolve that issue? This can happen through conversations with the student council. Provide them with specific examples of how your team uses student input in decision-making.

When it comes to this tension that plays out in context beliefs, we need to remember that an instructional leadership team (ILT), and the school to which it belongs, is filled with complex relationships. The success of these relationships is partly based on whether individuals feel supported by one another, whether those individuals work together to support their district, and ultimately, whether all of these actions contribute to a more supportive school and district culture.

I did not always keep this tension in mind when I was a school principal. There were times when I was upset that our staff was not getting the support they needed but I didn't always think about whether I was truly supporting the school district in their efforts either.

Dimmock and Walker (2002, p. 70) write, "Culture forms the context in which school leadership is exercised. It thus exerts a considerable influence on how school leaders think and act." Miller (2018, p. 6) writes "that the peculiarities of context shape the behavior of school leaders, and that successful school leaders adapt their leadership to the needs, opportunities and constraints within their own work contexts."

Given the fact that culture forms the context, it's no surprise that teachers and leaders within school districts have become increasingly skeptical when it comes to believing whether their districts will support them. This happens even when district office administration is the one who initiates the initiative because teachers and leaders do not believe that those in the district office will provide them with the resources they need to be successful.

That lack of belief is due in part because of ill-fated innovations or initiatives. Earlier in the book, the Boston Consulting Group Study was mentioned, and Hargreaves and O'Connor (2018b) wrote about how teachers felt that PLCs were the most disliked form of collaboration, and yet, school leaders were highly supportive of the process. That shows how complex context beliefs can be when it comes to how different stakeholders perceive a process that they believe is supportive or not.

A study by the Education Week Research Center (2019) found that "86% of school leaders completely agree that they support teachers who start innovative work or new initiatives." However, when teachers where asked the same question, only "45% of teachers agreed that their leaders support them when they begin innovative work or new initiatives." Does the staff you lead feel that you support their innovative efforts? How can you develop a more robust culture of innovation in your school?

Ford et al. (2020, p. 267) write, "Motivation is a complex, multidimensional construct that attempts to describe and explain the process by which goal-directed behavior is initiated, sustained, changed, and/or stopped." Leithwood and Mascall (2008) found that motivation is impacted by the agency that teachers feel in their buildings, districts, divisions, and boards, and agency is impacted by their capacity beliefs (i.e., sense of efficacy) and their context beliefs (see Figure 4.1).

Let's take a moment here to process this information that I just laid out. We know that context beliefs include whether teachers and leaders feel that their school building or district will support their efforts, but as I mentioned using the research from Dimmock, teachers and leaders also have to understand that they need to show support for their building or district at times. I would like you to consider both of those perspectives on support and context beliefs.

Figure 4.1 Capacity and Context Beliefs

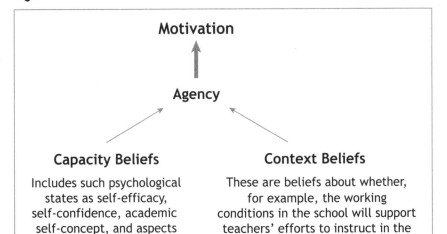

Leithwood, K., & Mascall, B. (2008). Collective leadership effects on student achievement. *Educational Administration Quarterly, 44*(4), 529-561.

REFLECT

Take a few moments to reflect individually, with a partner, or with your ILT.

● As a teacher or leader, was there a time when you did not feel supported in your efforts to be innovative? Provide an example.

● Was there a time when you *did* feel supported in your efforts to be innovative? Provide an example.

● What was the reason you were not supported in one effort and yet supported in the other? Were there any contributing factors that you can remember?

● Think about the level of support you give to others. Has there been a time when you were not supportive in an initiative within your building or district? Please provide an example.

(Continued)

(Continued)

● Has there been a time when you were supportive in an initiative within your building or district? Please provide an example.

● What was the reason you were not supportive in one effort and but were supportive in the other? Were there any contributing factors that you can remember?

We spend a lot of time focusing on when we are not supported and not enough time looking at our own behavior to learn why we are not supportive of others. For drivers such as context beliefs to work, we need to focus not only on what we don't get in a situation but also on our own behavior during these times. Additionally, context beliefs mean that we sometimes have to shift our behavior to match with the direction the school building or district may be going in. Instead of instant resistance, we have to understand how what we are doing already may fit in with that new direction.

 **NOTES**

NURTURING CONTEXT BELIEFS

I want to provide some practical context here. Anne-Marie Duguid and Julian Drinkall of the Academies Enterprise Trust (AET) in London offer some specific guidance about how they approach the complicated topic of context beliefs at AET.

FOUR PHASES OF CONTEXTUAL IMPROVEMENT

by Anne-Marie Duguid and Julian Drinkall
Academies Enterprise Trust, London UK
[2021]

Academies Enterprise Trust (AET) is one of the largest multi-academy trusts in England, with 58 schools. It is the only national trust with schools across all phases of education, aged 3-18. This piece explores the phases of turnaround within AET, including the preconditions needed to ensure that our teams and schools could thrive at scale; at the same time, we find a balance between allowing teachers and leaders to be innovative while focusing on the crisis we were experiencing when it comes to student learning.

A Little Bit About the Context

In the English model of schooling, some schools have become academies and formed groups called *multi-academy trusts.* Previously, as part of the strive toward the school-led system, AET grew too quickly and lost its sense of identity and "oneness." There was a mixture of teachers and leaders who were making their own decisions that were contrary to what students need and those teachers and leaders who were feeling lost because they lacked direction.

At its largest, AET led 77 academies but started to show signs of weakness in 2013-2014; academic results were in decline and the governance was broken or ineffective. The Department for Education in England lost faith in the trust and AET was often targeted by the media, politicians, and anti-academy groups.

Turnaround Was Needed

Trust leader Julian Drinkall (co-author) was appointed, and the turnaround started through a planned phase approach. Julian's underlying belief is that "AET is a huge and diverse organization, and every child (our current 43,000 and the future generation) is deserving of the same amount of high-quality support and the best possible education." Every member of staff needs to find how they best contribute to that aim. Today's and tomorrow's generation of pupils are and will be in our hands. The question became, how do teachers and leaders need to understand how their actions support the aim of the trust?

Under new leadership, turnaround has happened at scale and pace over the last four years. AET is now becoming the place to come and the place to stay.

How?

This is a journey that could apply at a single school or be scalable across school systems. It has been achieved in phases and it is important to note that each phase required a different set of leadership styles and behaviors.

> **Phase 1: Survival.** Leadership; building teams and skillset; top down; all about today, today, today
>
> **Phase 2: Building.** Visioning, focus on today but with tomorrow in view
>
> **Phase 3: Empowering.** Subtle judgement; focus on today, tomorrow, and the future
>
> **Phase 4: Everyone a leader.** The future, the five-year strategy kick-started

Phase 1: Survival

This was mainly traditional leadership and was very action orientated because of the dire need. AET felt like a toxic space with little trust and an absence of skills across the organization. The role of the trust leader became central. It required top-down survival leadership. Sleeves were firmly rolled up and some tough decisions were needed; it was a lonely place to lead. A lot of decisions were made; sometimes they were wrong or the timing was not quite right. However, in survival leadership, the biggest crime would have been not to take decisive action.

There were some immediate priorities needed before time could be spent developing the collective:

- Arrest financial freefall
- Consolidation
- Professionalize governance
- Kick-start school improvement
- Assemble a world-class, tight-knit, loyal team

Restructuring based on financials and skill sets was required, and there were a large number of losers. The importance of leading with integrity was essential. There was no sugarcoating of the pill, as the organization was in crisis mode. There was honesty about things that were not good enough, and high standards were set leading toward the building stage.

Phase 2: Building

Phase 2 included a more inclusive and consultative style of leadership, building and expanding the team's core to turnaround, and expanding technical skills and expertise while embracing more diversity and a lot more personalities. Teachers and leaders began to engage their voices in decision-making and started to feel a sense of agency. Getting the basics right in Phase 1 meant we earned the privilege and luxury of jointly discussing vision and values. We could start building the foundations and teams that were technical/adaptive and value based.

To do this, some structures needed to change and some preconditions needed to be laid:

- New board and executive team
- New governance model in 2017
- Ensure that the AET is financially secure
- All phases show year-on-year improvement
- 72% of academies are now rated good or outstanding (compared to 29% when they joined)

We could then develop a new vision, mission, and values in 2019 based on the voices of students, teachers, and leaders. This was an exciting journey; by working with a poet and external branding experts alongside our school leaders, the vision, mission, and values were collectively shaped. But, most importantly, they were defined and shaped at the local level by our children, staff, and community. This created a great sense of agency among the community.

A renewed sense of purpose and a real OneAET new identity emerged. The order mattered; it was essential to engage with employees rather than bypass them. We had to gain the trust of school leaders and the confidence that together, we can do this; we could have that collective belief that it was truly possible to develop remarkable children and remarkable staff for a remarkable world.

> **Our Vision:** *Each and every child is inspired to choose a remarkable life.*

> **Our Mission:** *To gather and motivate inspirational people committed to delivering an excellent education that launches children into remarkable lives*

Our Values:

Be unusually brave: At AET, we choose to be unusually brave. We're not afraid to challenge wrongs or to make the right call, even when it's both unusual and difficult to do so.

Push the limits: We always strive to push the limits. We don't settle for less than excellent and we won't allow our students to do so either. We resolve to overcome any self-imposed limits.

Discover what's possible: We are on the search for discovering what's possible. We look to create "eureka moments" for our students, helping them discover a world of possibilities and opportunities.

Be bighearted: We commit to being bighearted. We choose to treat each other with kindness, warmth, and care, believing that everybody matters and believing in one another.

There was a sea change of a different approach and a different path. Our OneAET identity clearly manifested in our first remarkable festival, with representation from across the country. The comment was heard, "I never thought it would be possible to get that community feel at such a scale, but what I am witnessing now is special and you can really see and feel it."

Phase 3: Empowering

In this phase, there were higher standards and good people—the raw materials needed to enact our vision and make it real within the individual school contexts. This also coincided with COVID and lockdown. But because the initial two phases' foundations were laid, there was a strong galvanizing of collective purpose. People listened to each other more and empathy fueled the discussions. A real team was coming together with a collective aim and an understanding of everyone's needs.

In many ways, COVID brought us closer and made everyone realize the advantage of working as part of a larger organization. There was a strong sense of connectedness; our leaders were not alone at a very scary time. Initially, this connection was through daily virtual briefings.

The next priority was to invest in laptops so that every child had a device and access to broadband to keep learning from being lost, especially for our most vulnerable pupils. Equity of access for all was key in our quest for social justice. We made sure all of our pupils had food on the holidays before the government stepped in. We focused on living out our values.

What else could we do to take the pain and pressure away? Immediate technical and pedagogical professional development was offered so everyone could teach online and focus on the learning. Systems were put in place to support and alleviate pressure on schools so they could focus on the learning. Collectively, the AET Virtual Learning Academy was created with open access for the larger education system (not only for our schools). Our mindset and belief was one of well-being and "we can do this together." The answers came from the group and were no longer about the individual.

The trust leader role at this stage changes; it is about subtle judgement. It is all about getting the balance right at an emotional and very difficult time; the balance between needing to be reassuring, calming, and accepting but also to challenge others to rise to the occasion. There is also the need to feel the pulse, to find out what is needed today versus tomorrow and to avoid exhaustion/burnout.

We liken this to surfing and being ahead of the curve: You train and you research to be ready for the wave. The productive collective instinctively know their roles not through a chain of command but through collective efficacy becoming a living and breathing reality. Resourcefulness is poised and ready to cope with uncertainty; everyone is well prepared and confident while sufficiently calm and anchored.

This has been truly humbling to witness and be a part of such selflessness.

And Now?

Phase 4: Everyone a Leader

In this stage, everyone is a leader. There is so much trust, and teams come together with an instinctive understanding between them. People self-select for roles with clear communication between all. Every part of AET is working as one: people, systems, curriculum, technology, pupils, communication, parents, and so on.

We are ready for the next phase—the five-year strategy has launched.

We have learned and continue to learn lessons from COVID, and we are excited about the future:

- School doesn't always have to be in the building within set hours.

- Teaching doesn't always have to be in-person, and staff and pupils can link between different locations.

- Adaptive technology can help increase teacher impact and reduce workload.

- Exciting new staff roles may emerge.

- Continuing to check-in with each and every child is important.

- There is power in a curriculum that's about every aspect of a child and young person.

The tide has changed; it is an exciting time to be part of AET.

Our new five-year strategy centers around self, academics, and pathways. We will get there by ensuring that we offer the best professional development and learning experiences for all our staff through the AET Institute—and that this is also facilitated by the staff within AET. We will build support for parents as we develop our virtual school, and we are committed to sustainability. We are very proud of our equality, equity, diversity, and inclusion (EEDI) work at staff and student levels. We have engaged with national external experts, created a global majority aspiring leadership program for our leaders, and provided heads and senior leaders with support and coaching to understand unconscious bias and our initial four pillars: disability, race and ethnicity, remarkable women, and sexual orientation and gender identity. We are setting up affinity and advisory groups from across our staff body to help in providing safe spaces and a voice. We are reviewing our curriculum through an EEDI lens. There is a cultural shift and mindset change from deficit thinking through raised awareness and dialogue.

We will make mistakes; we don't have all the answers but we have a chance to build a better future post-COVID and provide a remarkable education.

*https://www.gov.uk/government/publications/multi-academy-trusts-establishing-and-developing-your-trust

HOW SCHOOL DISTRICTS AND DIVISIONS CAN ENHANCE CONTEXT BELIEFS

Just as within the AET context, school districts can enhance the context beliefs of school leaders and their team members by understanding a few specific areas. Those areas are locus of control, a voice in the process, ongoing professional learning and development, leadership coaching, and conditional autonomy. What we know is that teachers may not feel supported by their school principals; therefore, they have a negative view where context beliefs are concerned. However, the same negative view can take place for school leaders if they feel they are working in a district or division where they do not feel supported. There are five areas that will help teachers and leaders deepen their understanding around context. Feeling supported is easy because we clearly see when we get what we want. It's when we don't feel supported that is rough for us because we feel we are not getting what we want. The five areas addressed here are ways that we can better understand our context beliefs because they provide us with a deeper picture of our current reality.

WHERE SOURCES OF EFFICACY INTERSECT WITH CONTEXT BELIEFS

Mastery Experiences

- **Leadership coaching.** Leadership coaching can provide a mastery experience for school leaders to work with an experienced coach who can be a nonjudgmental listener in the process. The combined report by the Learning Policy Institute and National Association of Secondary School Principals (NASSP, 2020, p. 6) found that "both mentors and coaches provide critical learning opportunities for principals. Principals often report that having a mentor or coach is the most valuable learning opportunity for them."

  - Leadership coaching can help enhance the context beliefs of individuals and teams because through the experience the individuals and teams can see that their voice matters and their district or division cares about their success, and they develop a deeper impact on learning.

Ask Conceptual Questions. When confronted with new initiatives, ask the following questions:

- What is the relationship between this initiative and what we are already doing?

- How does this initiative fit in with our present actions?

- How does what we are doing already accomplish this (so we do not have to take on yet another initiative)?

- **Cycles of inquiry.** Engaging in a cycle of inquiry can be difficult because of the conversations that are necessary to the process, but through the cycle of inquiry, conversations regarding context beliefs are present and can help members of the ILT see where they fit into the greater good.

Vicarious Experiences

- **Ongoing professional learning and development.** Ongoing professional learning and development will establish coherence within the district or board and then each specific school building. Fullan and Quinn (2016, p. 1) define *coherence* as "the shared depth of understanding about the purpose and nature of the work." Coherence will help districts and divisions develop a common language and common understanding around the goals

(Continued)

(Continued)

that are being established. By doing this, districts and building leaders can work together to take out some of the ambiguity that comes with initiative fatigue and may clear up misunderstandings that contribute to negative context beliefs that exist between teachers and leaders. Ongoing professional learning and development at its core is meant to clear up the context between goals and actions. The key word here is *ongoing*, because we know that "sit and get" is not impactful, and ongoing professional development has been found to be more impactful (Timperley et al., 2007).

- **Partner schools.** When implementing or de-implementing initiatives, encourage schools within the district to develop partnerships so they can learn from one another. Our context beliefs can be skewed by myopic thinking; working in partnership with another school can broaden our view.

Social Persuasion

- **Locus of control.** We often get frustrated by those things that are outside of our control. This is where well-being and mental health are critical because the study of mindfulness practices helps us to understand what we can control and what is outside of our sphere of influence. Michael Fullan once said in a keynote, "Just because you're stuck with their policies, doesn't mean you need to be stuck with their mindsets." Using the conceptual questions from above will go a long way toward helping people understand their locus of control and will help us engage in discussions where we, as leaders, can offer others the emotional support they need. Bandura (1997, p. 101) writes, "It is easier to sustain a sense of efficacy, especially when struggling with difficulties, if significant others express faith in one's capabilities than if they convey doubts."

- **Voice.** When it comes to some defined actions that districts can take, Ford et al. (2020, pp. 273, 279) found that there are several ways in which districts can support the context beliefs of school leaders. The important aspect to the following is that building leaders have a voice in the process of defining goals for not only their buildings but also for their districts or divisions.

If district leaders talk *at* building leaders and not *with* building leaders, positive context beliefs will not be created. There are times that districts may need to dictate the goal due to being flagged by their states or ministries (i.e., Canada, Australia, etc.) for low test scores with English language learners or low math scores among their special education population or Black and brown student populations. In those cases, a district may need to dictate the goal, but how the ILT goes about achieving the goal may be up to them. The voice in the process comes when districts define the goal but building leaders and teachers define how to address the goal.

Affective States

- **Conditional autonomy.** Ford et al. (2020) also found a "robust body of evidence regarding the critical role of autonomy in fostering principal success" (p. 273). I do want to offer a cautionary tale when looking at autonomy. *Autonomy* is one of those words that we need to develop a common language and common understanding around. I write that because to some, autonomy means being left alone and getting what they want.

What we want is the happy medium, where we feel we have a voice in the process but also understand that we no longer live in the days when we can do whatever we want. Autonomy means understanding the goal of our district and then being able to be creative within that goal. It's not about thinking outside the box as much as it is being creative within the box.

Teachers and leaders may often feel that they are not getting what they want and then yell, "We have no autonomy!" in resistance to it all. Conditional autonomy means we understand that we work in a building or district where there need to be goals, and our conditional autonomy comes in the form of how we individually address those goals. Once again, the conceptual questions listed above can help in this process.

IN THE END

To function effectively as an ILT, we need to understand the role of context beliefs. It is hard to be motivated on an individual or team basis if we do not believe our voice is valued. As leaders, we often want our voices to be valued within our district, and that means we should take the necessary steps to ensure that the voices of our ILTs are valued as well.

Context beliefs are much more complicated than simply feeling that we got what we wanted. Sometimes what we want does not fit into

> Sometimes what we want does not fit into the greater good of the district—in fact, it may take important resources away from that greater good—and that is where tension is created.

the greater good of the district—in fact, it may take important resources away from that greater good—and that is where tension is created. It's important that as an ILT, you fully understand the nuances of context beliefs.

When people understand the role of context beliefs, they are more likely to have a clearer and more holistic vision of their working conditions, which is the focus of Chapter 5. All these drivers are interrelated. As a team, select a few drivers to focus on together.

GUIDING QUESTIONS

- What is the relationship between context beliefs and motivating individuals and a team?
- When have there been times that you felt supported to engage in innovative practices?
- When have there been times you did not feel supported to engage in innovative practices?
- When have there been times when your school building or district could say their context beliefs were not supported by you?
- In what ways can districts support the context beliefs of school leaders?

What two questions do you wish I had asked?

1.

2.

What three new areas of learning did you experience while reading this chapter?

1.

2.

3.

NOTES

WORKING CONDITIONS

5

The definition of insanity is doing the same thing over and over again and expecting a different result.

(This quote is often attributed to Albert Einstein, but research shows he didn't say it.)

THEORY OF ACTION

If . . . we understand the characteristics of our working conditions, then . . . we will be able to take actionable steps to improve our working conditions.

GUIDING QUESTIONS

- When building collective leader efficacy, why is it necessary to understand working conditions?

- In what ways do leaders in your school contribute positively to the working conditions of teachers?

- In what ways do you contribute negatively to your own working conditions?

- How could de-implementation improve your working conditions?

- According to Rui Yan, what are the four elements that contribute to working conditions?

- Which one of those elements uses language that we need to change?

- How can your instructional leadership team have a positive impact on the working conditions of others in the school?

WORKING CONDITIONS

Working conditions have a major impact on our lives. When the working conditions are positive, we feel connected and as if we are a part of something greater than ourselves. When they are negative, they contribute to our stress, which can sometimes feel insurmountable. We often don't see how we control our working conditions as much as we believe they control us.

> We often don't see how we control our working conditions as much as we believe they control us.

In my 11 years as a teacher, I worked for many types of principals, most of whom were more managers than instructional leaders, and a couple of those ran the building with an iron fist mentality. When Robinson (2008) wrote about leaders who use coercion, force, and manipulation, I could definitely identify. There were some who could be engaging and friendly one day but angry and combative the next. One had almost manic behavior and would walk in and out of formal observations because they felt like it, only to ask questions during the post-observation conversation that would have been answered if they had remained in the classroom. The reality is that as a teacher, I actually only believed that a principal was a manager and never expected them to be a partner in my learning.

Although I respected most of the leaders I worked with, and they certainly had their positive traits, I tried to stay out of their way. The classroom was my refuge, the place I could partner with students, so it's really not a surprise to me that many teachers close the door and want to work within their own silo. Many times, it's safer in there.

The International Labour Organization (2015) says, "Working conditions are at the core of paid work and employment relationships. Generally speaking, working conditions cover a broad range of topics and issues, from working time (hours of work, rest periods, and work schedules) to remuneration, as well as the physical conditions and mental demands that exist in the workplace."

When it comes to the specific working conditions within a school, Johnson (2006) gives more details of teacher working conditions:

> The physical features of buildings, organizational structures that define teachers' formal positions and relationships with others in the school, sociological features that shape how teachers experience their work, political features of their organization, cultural features of the school as a workplace that influence teachers' interpretation

of what they do and their commitment, psychological features of the environment that may sustain or deplete them personally, [and] educational features, such as curriculum and testing policies, that may enhance or constrain what teachers can teach. (p. 2)

What we know from research and our personal experience is that the school leader is one of the biggest factors that contribute to the working conditions of a school (Burkhauser, 2017; Ladd, 2011). As you read in some of my experiences as a teacher, we can definitely understand how principals can impact our working conditions. As a school principal for eight years, I understood deeply how I impacted the working conditions of teachers and staff within the school I led because I knew how the principal impacted me when I was a teacher. I worked hard to foster a climate of partnership among teachers and staff, but it wasn't easy because the other working conditions in the district were not always positive and I had to learn how to negotiate my way through those times.

Take a moment here to engage in a deliberate practice conversation with your instructional leadership team (ILT). It should not take more than 10 minutes to do this activity, but it's important to discuss the positive aspects of your working conditions.

WORKING CONDITIONS

List the top three reasons why the working conditions in your school are positive. If your school climate is hostile, then feel free to name three reasons why that is, but I'm hoping you will be able to focus on the positive.

1.

2.

3.

What role do you play in helping to create positive working conditions?

Thank you for taking the time to do the activity. If you are being open and honest, I'm sure these are not easy questions to engage in. What's interesting about most of the research on school working conditions is that it is focused on how the teacher is made to feel within a school and usually shows the teacher on the receiving end of it all. What about the school leader? How do working conditions impact the school principal?

WORKING CONDITIONS FOR LEADERS

Yan (2020, p. 93) writes, "Working conditions serve as the core of work and employment relationships, covering a broad range of topics from working time, remuneration, to physical conditions and mental demands that exist in the workplace." Using all the preexisting research, Yan goes on to write that there are "four major dimensions of principal working conditions: (a) job benefits, (b) workload, (c) school disciplinary environment, and (d) principal influences on school matters" (p. 96). For full disclosure, I do not like the wording "school disciplinary environment" because I believe it focuses on the negative. This language can create a dynamic that fosters the deficit thinking I addressed in Chapter 2. ILTs should work together to change such destructive language from one that focuses on negative behaviors to language that fosters more inclusive behavior. We would do well to change school disciplinary environment to inclusive school climate.

I understand that the point of Yan's research was to address how discipline issues impact a leader's desire to stay in that particular school. However, if leaders can begin to change their mindset, and the mindsets of others, to look at some discipline issues as a lack of engagement, then they would be more likely to stay because they will see the issue not as being reactive (discipline) but as being proactive (inclusivity and engagement).

There has been a correlation between working conditions and school leadership turnover (Mitani, 2018). Although student relationships are the most important factors for those of us who serve or served in the role of school building leader, research does show that if school leaders do not see their salary and benefits as competitive compared to peers in other school districts, it will be a major factor that contributes to them leaving their school district (Pijanowski & Brady, 2009).

The impact of salary also relates to the workload of school leaders. If school leaders see their workload as consistently increasing with no additional benefits contributing to their compensation, as well as the increase in workload constantly taking them away from their families, they are less likely to stay on their job.

Workload is an important factor for school leaders—and not only due to salary. In a 10-year study by the National Association for Elementary School Principals (NAESP), Fuller et al. (2018, p. 3) found that it is becoming increasingly difficult to fill principal positions, "citing a salary not commensurate with responsibilities, time demands of the job, an ever-increasing workload, and stress as factors that could discourage good candidates." How exactly does the amount of stress that leaders feel impact how students feel? How might student councils help alleviate some of that stress? Pause here for a Student Council Reflection.

STUDENT COUNCIL REFLECTION

If leaders are stressed in your school, how does that negatively impact students? Does it mean less time spent listening to student voice? How could student councils help alleviate some of the stress that comes with the working conditions within a school?

Student councils may be able to offer valuable insight into how to improve the working conditions within their school community. Whether it's engaging them in an instructional leadership meeting or surveying their input, student councils can offer specific suggestions on how to improve the working conditions.

In a study of secondary school principals, Klocko and Wells (2015, p. 332) found that "the workload of principals continues to increase with new expectations for evaluation and supervision, changing legislative mandates, and mounting pressures." This is not only a problem in the United States. In a recent study of principals by the New South Wales Department of Education in Australia (2017, p. 4), researchers found that "principals have reported their increased administrative workload is preventing them from fulfilling their core responsibilities as educational leaders." The researchers went on to say the following:

> Most principals reported that they consider their current workload to be unreasonable. While they acknowledged that working beyond standard hours is required to undertake their role, there is a general

feeling that the current workload is neither achievable (75% reporting that their workload is "difficult to achieve" or "not at all achievable") nor sustainable in the longer term (77% reporting that their workload is "difficult to sustain" or "not at all sustainable"). (p. 5)

In a report sponsored by the Organization for Economic Cooperation and Development (OECD) of school leaders in developed countries around the world, Pont et al. (2008, p. 15) write, "In recent years, the workload of school leaders has expanded and intensified as a result of increased school autonomy and accountability for learning outcomes. . . . This workload goes beyond what one single individual can possibly achieve successfully."

It's due to increased workloads that I offer up research focusing on de-implementation throughout this book. Wang et al. (2017, pp. 2-3) write, "De-implementation comes down to four areas. Those areas are:

- Partial reduction

- Complete reversal

- Substitution with related replacement

- Substitution with unrelated replacement of existing practice."

De-implementation takes a level of unlearning on the part of an individual or team. Wang et al. (2017, p. 3) go on to write,

Unlearning is a process of discarding outdated mental models to make room for alternative models. In each of the four types of change described above, change requires effort to learn new knowledge and to unlearn what was thought to be effective. Moreover, the relative efforts required for learning and unlearning vary by the type of change.

Although the process of de-implementation and unlearning may seem like a great deal of heavy lifting, the reality is that the process of unlearning can be used on all future implementations to help teams decide what initiatives are no longer necessary within their school community.

For example, I worked with a group of leadership teams in Massachusetts a few years ago and we engaged in a discussion about school climate. One middle school principal who was at the workshop with his school-based team, which included teachers and a school psychologist, was convinced that they needed to establish a new team to focus on school climate. When I suggested the very team he sat with could do the work, he honestly said that he was with his school leadership team and they didn't do school climate work and that they needed a new school climate team to do the work.

This is a problem among schools. Instead of taking time to conceptually understand how the same actions can help solve a variety of problems, too many school leaders believe they have to create new committees to solve each individual issue. This process of getting leaders to stop this behavior requires unlearning. Let's take a moment here to reflect about de-implementation in your school.

Activity 5.1 What Could Be De-Implemented?

Take a moment with your team to write a list of initiatives or actions on the left side of the table you would like to de-implement within your school. On the right side of the table, consider the unlearning that needs to take place. I will start the list for you.

Initiative/Action to De-implement	Unlearning Necessary to Consider
Too many committees	We want to unlearn that there needs to be a committee for every new initiative or issue happening within our school community. This does not mean get rid of all committees, but it does mean we have to seriously consider which ones should remain.
Content in classrooms	During the COVID pandemic, many teachers condensed the content being taught and focused on vital standards. We need to unlearn our dependency on factual knowledge and engage in conceptual knowledge learning, which provides the opportunity to offer deeper learning experiences while using less content.

(Continued)

(Continued)

Initiative/Action to De-implement	Unlearning Necessary to Consider

In order to seriously take action on our workloads, we need to engage in new behaviors that will allow us to de-implement at the same time we consider implementation. We often add more and more initiatives to our plates but we do not spend adequate time deciding what can come off our plates.

According to Yan, besides workload, there are additional factors that contribute to working conditions, such as a high number of student discipline issues and the school leader's feeling that they cannot do anything to change it. This is why the context beliefs addressed in Chapter 4 are important. If school leaders feel they have a voice in how they can address issues such as student discipline and feel they have more control over their workload, it will begin to contribute to a more positive perspective on their working conditions.

So, although workload, salary, and student discipline are vitally important, we need to look at the larger umbrella of working conditions to begin to make positive improvements in our buildings and districts. And contrary to our popular belief, we *do* have some control over the conditions in which we work. The simple fact is that the report from OECD is correct, that leaders cannot do it all on their own, but even deeper than that, in some cases, leaders do not have to keep doing all that they are doing.

Whether you are a school building leader, assistant principal, teacher leader, instructional coach, counselor, school psychologist, or any other role on the ILT, please consider tracking a week of your time. Appendix 3 shows a weekly log that was created for you to use when trying to gain an understanding of how you spend your time. This will only work if you are honest, and you don't have to use the form I have provided. Feel free to just use a notebook. I want you to get a sense of where you devote your energy during one week. I track my progress on workouts and what I eat in order to maintain a healthy lifestyle and it has worked well for me. I hope this will work for you.

If we don't learn to control our time, then time will control us. I'm not debating that some days are much tougher than others. What I am debating is whether that should happen as often as it does. This is an important conversation when it comes to workload, because identifying where you spend your time will go a long way in providing you insight into when and whether you can practice instructional leadership. It's one way that you can begin to take back control of working conditions. Now, let's identify some other ways.

IMPROVE YOUR WORKING CONDITIONS

When it comes to workload, there are many benefits to moving away from the mindset that leaders have to do everything on their own and moving to a mindset of collaboration. Sometimes we are our own worst enemies and make our jobs harder because we try to do everything on our own and reinvent the wheel for each initiative. Working collaboratively with others doesn't mean getting others to do the work; it means combining our best thinking so we can take on our greatest issues together. This takes openness and vulnerability on the part of the school leader. Too many leaders put on a brave face and try to operate daily as if everything is fine, but we know that we are not always fine.

The question of how we improve our working conditions begins by being open and honest with each other and encouraging that openness and honesty from our staff, which ultimately contributes to how our ILTs interact with one another and build collective leader efficacy together. We need to affirm that we can improve our working conditions, but it means that leaders and teachers will have to reflect on their actions, stop being martyrs who believe they can only do it alone, and begin setting boundaries. Using Yan's (2020) research on the four elements that contribute to working conditions—(1) job benefits, (2) workload, (3) school disciplinary environment, and (4) principal influences on school matters—I wanted to offer a deeper perspective on each. As you read through the list and descriptions I have offered in Activity 5.1, consider your relationship with each element. There is a blank spot for you to write down your own thoughts.

 # Activity 5.2 How Can We Improve Our Working Conditions?

The following are suggestions on improving workload. All of these suggestions fit into the efficacy experiences that Bandura (1997) found to increase our level of efficacy.

1. **Job Benefits**

    ● **Salary.** Salary is merely one part of the job, albeit a very
       important part. Clearly, working with a state leadership
       organization to help make sure a leader's salary is competitive
       with similar school districts is important. As a principal, our K-12
       building leadership collective worked together to negotiate a
       more competitive salary

Write your own thoughts:

    ● **Student relationships.** Working in a great community, engaging
       with students, and seeing growth are some of the greatest benefits
       of this job. In this past year, I officiated the wedding of two of my
       former first graders—even though it had been more than 20 years
       since I had seen them in person (we were friends on social media).
       As teachers and leaders, we may spend a year or more with
       students, but they remember us forever. Will it be a good or bad
       memory for them?

Write your own thoughts:

(Continued)

(Continued)

- **Innovation.** One of the benefits of school leadership is the ability to be innovative and have some control over our own working conditions as well as the ability to foster that same spirit of innovation in our teachers and students.

Write your own thoughts:

2. **Workload**

- **Set boundaries.** I was controlled by my phone for so long. I felt like it was my duty to check email every hour on the hour while I was at home. Then I began setting boundaries; I stopped checking email after a certain time of day and talked with staff about doing the same. Our profession is important but so is our chance to have a personal life.

How will you do this in your own practices?

- **Reflect on your use of time.** Leaders need to be honest about how they spend their time. What tasks take up your day?

What are your thoughts on how you spend your time?

- **Frameworks.** In *Collaborative Leadership* (DeWitt, 2016) and *Instructional Leadership* (DeWitt, 2020a), I included reflective frameworks. The Australian Institute for Teaching and School Leadership (AITSL) also has a great framework. These frameworks can be used for evidence-based reflection and can assist leaders in understanding where they can best spend their time and may help them understand where they should not spend time at all.

Do you use frameworks to help you remain focused?

- **Change the physical environment.** When I was a principal, our teachers used theatre gels that covered some of the fluorescent lights to provide softer lighting. Some teachers used lamps. Bringing in elements of home, using student artwork all over the building, and finding ways to utilize natural light were some great ways to change the physical environment.

What are ways you have improved your physical environment?

3. **School Disciplinary Environment**

- **Address negativity.** If we recorded our daily conversations, I bet we would be surprised by how negative conversations can be. Negative language eats away at a positive school climate. We address this through conversations at faculty and staff meetings. We also address it during one-on-one conversations with people who are negative quite often. If we allow negativity to go unchecked, we contribute to a negative school climate.

(Continued)

(Continued)

How do you prevent or disrupt negative talk among others or with yourself?

● **Focus on student engagement.** Odetola et al. (1972) found that students are disengaged from school because they (a) lack an emotional connection to their teacher or school community and (b) feel they do not have a voice in their own learning. Student discipline issues can come from a lack of engagement. Focusing on engagement can help alleviate some of these discipline issues.

In what ways do you engage students?

The following three suggestions are offered by Hannigan and Hannigan (2016):

Belief. As educators, we approach instruction with the belief that every student can and will learn. With this belief, we exhaust every resource and support necessary to improve learning. As an administrator, you have to question your own beliefs about discipline. Do you believe every student can and will behave decently? Is every resource and strategy exhausted to support a student in their behavior, or is suspension used as the only means to teach a student how to behave? If you believe what you are currently doing is working, then there is no compelling reason to change. If you do not believe in preventive discipline, it will not be an expectation nor a priority in your school.

Visibility and active supervision. As an administrator, it is vital to be out of your office and visible to students and staff in order to build effective relationships and make meaningful connections with students. Active supervision requires an intentional focus on movement, scanning, and positive interactions during supervision; this is essential and needs to be modeled by the administrator. Taking the time to train your staff on visibility and active supervision will save you the time of responding to behavior incidents due to deficiencies in supervision from staff.

Invest in gaining faculty commitment. Take time to educate your staff on alternative discipline approaches. Make it a priority to share school behavior data, gather input from the staff, and work with staff on discipline so they feel that they have a voice in the process. Share effective discipline success stories with the staff. If you take the time to do this and make yourself available to have difficult ongoing conversations around beliefs, you will see more ownership by staff when handling minor discipline and increased collective ownership on major administrator-handled discipline. Communication is also key for staff to understand the logic behind conducting behavior in this structure. In addition, discipline will become a team effort in supporting a student rather than something only executed and monitored by an administrator.

4. **Principal Influences on School Matters**

   - **Talk with one another.** I remember when email was new and we were all excited to have another way to communicate with people who might be far away. But due to our own laziness or need to get items off our lists, we email people who may be 100 feet away. Perhaps we can use the easy questions for email, but we need to save the deep topics (i.e., parent issues, union questions, negative responses, etc.) for one-on-one conversations. If we are in a hybrid or distance learning situation, we may want to consider using the phone or scheduling a Zoom or Meet. If we can't talk with one another, how can we ever collaboratively work together on a team?

Name a few ways in which you talk with your staff:

(Continued)

(Continued)

- **Proactive versus reactive.** As a principal, I looked for places where I was constantly being reactive and started to make changes to become more proactive. For example, when union reps wanted to stop me in the hallway to talk about issues, I began turning it around by creating a space where we could talk every Friday morning for an hour. If there was a crisis during the week when it came to the union, then we could talk immediately, but most issues were not a crisis and could wait until Friday morning. That helped me free up a lot of time.

Likewise, if discipline issues regularly occurred during recess, I proactively made myself available at recess or during lunch to walk around and give a before-recess talk to the students who often required discipline. I looked at the discipline data to understand which teachers had the most discipline issues and addressed those teachers. Often, we know where our problems are but deal with them reactively instead of proactively.

How do you focus on being proactive?

- **Communicate.** This was an area where I spent a great deal of time. I had to learn how to communicate more effectively. Too often, our working conditions are affected negatively because we don't communicate well. I made sure my emails were thoughtful or that I flipped my faculty meetings in an effort to provide everyone with information ahead of time that we could then dissect together.

What is your best form of communication that encourages dialogue?

Before we can move on to the other drivers, these four elements need a little more of our time and effort because they can be seen as barriers to how we move on as a team. For example, how many of us have said that our workloads have increased and we feel frustrated because of it?

In Activity 5.3, using the SWOT analysis method, consider the strengths, weaknesses, opportunities, and threats for each of the four elements of working conditions. The reasons for this activity are the following:

1. You need to see that you do have strengths and opportunities in each of these elements.

2. In order for your team to be proactive rather than reactive, it's important to really work together to articulate the weaknesses and threats that are barriers to your success.

3. The work here is to provide you with evidence that you can also bring to your district office to gain their assistance. I added a spot at the end of each SWOT analysis box for you to offer a suggestion on how your district can help you.

One final note before you engage in Activity 5.3: I changed the language on one of the elements (*student disciplinary environment*). I believe that language focuses on compliance and I would like to offer language that encourages voice, so I changed it to *inclusive student climate*.

Take some time to engage in this activity with your team.

Activity 5.3 SWOT Analysis

Your Working Conditions

1. Job Benefits

Job Benefits: SWOT Analysis

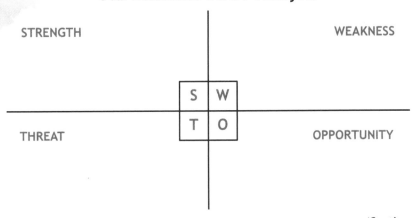

(Continued)

How can your school district assist you?

2. Workload

Workload: SWOT Analysis

STRENGTH   WEAKNESS

S	W
T	O

THREAT   OPPORTUNITY

How can your school district assist you?

3. Inclusive School Climate

Inclusive School Climate: SWOT Analysis

STRENGTH   WEAKNESS

S	W
T	O

THREAT   OPPORTUNITY

How can your school district assist you?

4. Principal Influences

Principal Influences: SWOT Analysis

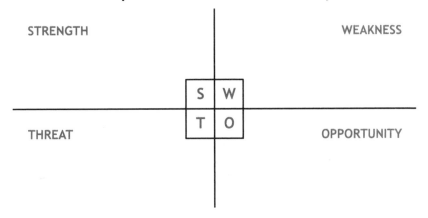

How can your school district assist you?

IN THE END

When we look at working conditions, we often focus on how outside influences impact our professional lives. Those outside influences may be the district office, the families of our students, or state and ministry accountability, and all of those are impactful for sure. However, we do not spend enough time looking at how our own actions impact our working conditions or how our words impact the working conditions of others.

If you're reading this book, then you are probably the kind of person who believes you never work hard enough or that you can do just one more thing to positively impact the people around you. I am one of those people as well. But it comes at a cost. That cost is sometimes our health or our relationships or both. We need to gain a deep understanding of what our working conditions are and then begin to establish boundaries to deal with those working conditions.

This leads to our next driver—professional learning and development. Use the understandings you have gained on mental health and well-being, context beliefs, and working conditions to collaboratively plan professional learning and development that enhances teacher and student voice and fosters growth in each member of the ILT.

GUIDING QUESTIONS

- When building collective leader efficacy, why is it necessary to understand working conditions?

- In what ways do leaders in your school contribute positively to the working conditions of teachers?

- In what ways do you contribute negatively to your own working conditions?

- How could de-implementation help improve your working conditions?

- According to Rui Yan, what are the four elements that contribute to working conditions?

- Which one of those elements uses language that we need to change?

- How can your instructional leadership team have a positive impact on the working conditions of others in the school?

What two questions do you wish I had asked?

1.

2.

What three new areas of learning did you experience
while reading this chapter?

1.

2.

3.

NOTES

PROFESSIONAL LEARNING AND DEVELOPMENT

6

When professional learning is interdependent, a teacher's individual success hinges on the efforts of the entire team.

Jenni Donohoo and Ann Mausbach (2021, p. 22)

THEORY OF ACTION

If . . . instructional leadership teams can develop a deeper understanding of what professional learning and development should look like, then . . . those teams can develop professional learning and development plans that will have a greater impact on the joint work taking place in school.

GUIDING QUESTIONS

- What is the difference between professional learning and professional development?

- What professional learning and development is needed for each individual on the team to be successful?

- What is the necessary professional learning and development your instructional leadership team needs to successfully have an impact on student learning?

WHAT IS PROFESSIONAL LEARNING AND DEVELOPMENT?

For full disclosure, I love professional learning and development. I realize that I should love it considering I facilitate workshops, but part of what I enjoy so much is listening to groups of people engaging in joint work around learning that will hopefully have an impact on student learning. I use the word *hopefully* because we know that there are many times when what people learn at a workshop or conference does not transition into actionable steps when they get back to school.

This inability to transition learning from a workshop to actionable steps is something I have wrestled with in my position of facilitator and is the reason I began offering a series of competency-based workshops; groups of people engaged in joint work but had to come back to the next workshop with evidence of how they utilized that learning. When COVID became a pandemic and my in-person workshops went remote, I created an eight-week online course to engage in joint work with participants and help them use that learning to have a greater impact at school, and a full-year on-demand course for instructional coaches, learning specialists, and leadership coaches in which coaches worked on their own cycle of inquiry as they helped leaders work on one. We developed a community together and learned from each other in the process.

My wrestling with effective professional learning and development is also one of the reasons why I am laying out such a comprehensive process throughout this book, which will end with your instructional leadership team (ILT) engaging in an inquiry cycle.

What we know is that professional learning and development is not only done through joint work. I am engaging in professional learning and development through writing this book because of the research that I am reading and the research I am engaged with as I work with school teams. You engage in professional learning and development in much the same way: by reading articles, learning from colleagues, through your learning walks, and engaging in off-site workshops. Professional learning and development does take some clarification, though, because in order to do it more effectively, we have to get a better sense of what it really is, and researchers in Canada have been doing very deep work around that topic.

Professional learning and *professional development* are often used interchangeably (Campbell et al., 2017), but the reality is that they are not the same thing. Fullan and Hargreaves (2017) write,

> Professional learning is often like student learning—something that is deliberately structured and increasingly accepted because it can (to some) more obviously be linked to measurable outcomes. In the teaching profession, these outcomes are often connected to teacher quality, performance, and impact just like student learning is often understood as student achievement. (p. 3)

Professional development is important as well and is slightly different from professional learning. Hargreaves and Fullan (2017, p. 4) write, "Professional development involves many aspects of learning but may also involve developing mindfulness, team building and team development, intellectual stimulation for its own sake, [and] reading good literature that prompts reflection on the human condition." In reading both definitions, we can understand the deep need for more professional learning and professional development and less training.

Le Fevre et al. (2020) write,

> Professional learning is often directed at teachers, particularly if the content focuses on teaching practices to promote student learning or well-being. On the surface, this approach appears to be logical because teachers have the greatest direct impact on student learning. Yet the research is clear; leaders who promote and participate in teacher [professional learning] PL and development have twice the effect size of other leadership activities. (p. 4)

Keep in mind Robinson's research (2008), which showed that leaders who promoted and participated in teacher learning had an effect size of .84; teacher learning was the leadership practice with the highest impact.

NOTES

PROFESSIONAL LEARNING AND DEVELOPMENT—NOT TRAINING

The research around drivers necessary for building collective leader efficacy focuses on that of leadership *training*. I have to admit that I disagree with that terminology. When we think of leadership training, we usually think about pre-service training for prospective leaders. I don't want leaders to be *trained* as much as I want them to focus on the learning they need to be successful. Training builds compliance; learning builds self-determination and growth.

> *Training builds compliance; learning builds self-determination and growth.*

Most people do not think that school building leaders need professional learning because those leaders have degrees and, in many cases, they also have a number of years of experience. Too often, school building leaders are perceived as people who have reached their pinnacle; they dictate the learning others should do. They are not seen as needing to be the recipients of learning. Nothing could be further from the truth.

In reports by Learning Forward, National Association of Secondary School Principals (NASSP), National Association for Elementary School Principals (NAESP), Australian Institute for Teaching and School Leadership (AITSL), and Organization for Economic Cooperation and Development (OECD), there has been a steady thread that runs through them all, and that is the need for ongoing professional growth for school leaders. If you are not in a leadership role, you may think that the need for ongoing learning is dictated by the district office, which is sometimes true. However, many school leaders admit that they want some level of control over their own learning to help them grow professionally and become more impactful leaders. They are no more done with their learning than a teacher is done with their learning, so a balance between what the district office wants all school leaders to learn (i.e., curriculum measures, gradual release of responsibility, a new data management tool, etc.) and what school building leaders need (i.e., an understanding of instructional leadership, how to build collective leader efficacy, etc.) to learn is key.

School-based leaders are often handed the keys to the building after they secure the job and are left to run the building while the district office holds them accountable for student improvement. They are given all of the tasks and increasing demands but are rarely ever given the professional development they need to continue to be successful at increasing student improvement. Too often, they have to attend professional development that is focused on the next thing their state education department may want or the next thing the superintendent believes is the new wave of education. There is an intersection between professional development and initiative fatigue, and it often takes place at the crossroads between what a state education department may believe school building leaders need and what school building leaders themselves believe they need.

Even school building leaders who have fresh degrees in leadership from a university program need to focus on professional growth, which often goes beyond what they learned at a university. Don't get me wrong, it's important to take classes that focus on educational law, principles of curriculum leadership, or critical issues when we are learning to be school leaders, but it's often difficult to remember what was said in a class two years prior and use it when we are actual school building leaders. There's a difference between learning about ideas in a self-contained class at night when we are teachers during the day than it is to actually try to put it into practice when we are the ones who have been handed the keys.

Therefore, the leadership professional growth I am referring to here is in-service leadership development because it takes place on the job and needs to take place with the very people who will be with leaders as they implement improvement. Cliff et al. (2018, p. 85) write,

> In-service leadership development is nuanced; there are intended activities as part of the process to equip individuals and build their capacity as they learn and adapt to shouldering responsibility and accountability. . . . While some development is instructed, developmental learning occurs both consciously and subconsciously through life and professional opportunities and experiences.

Those ongoing activities are what I'm offering in this book and asking you to work on from chapter to chapter. Ongoing and effective professional learning and development is necessary for everyone in a school leadership position. That means they need to be engaged in in-service leadership learning and development that will help them focus on aspects of instructional leadership, which will ultimately help their ILT. Instructional leadership has six different elements: implementation, a focus for learning, student engagement, instructional strategies, efficacy, and evidence of impact (DeWitt, 2020a).

PROFESSIONAL LEARNING AND DEVELOPMENT AS A DRIVER FOR COLLECTIVE LEADER EFFICACY

Effective professional learning and development is an important driver for both the school building leader and the team. ILTs are at risk of a top-down governance model, which ultimately will not build collective leader efficacy. The process of collective leader efficacy is about learning from one another and how that learning will have a positive impact on the student experience in a school. Unfortunately, as I stated earlier, school building leaders do not often learn together with their teachers, and for an effective ILT, learning together is a must.

As Le Fevre et al. (2020) found,

> Many leaders are reluctant to engage with teachers in new [professional learning] PL, and many do not have the necessary knowledge and skills to do so. Leadership and leadership development are seen as something different from working with teachers to improve student outcomes for students. The same situation often exists for district and policy leaders. They perceive it to be their job to determine the relevant policies, content, and approaches to PL and development rather than to engage with new learning themselves. (p. 4)

Of course, getting leaders and teachers to engage in learning together will take trust, and leaders will have to let down their guard when it comes to topics they may lack knowledge about. The reason why it's called *professional learning and development* is due to the fact that those who engage in it—teachers, staff, and leaders—are supposed to learn while they are there. Leaders are not immune to learning nor should they feel like they have to know it all in the first place.

Guskey (2021) suggests that there are six key ingredients in professional learning and development that will have staying power and will therefore be impactful:

1. **Focus on evidence-based practices.** Guskey says we should plan for learning that focuses on outcomes and not processes. That plan should be focused on student learning outcomes. Of course, without processes, there may not be any outcomes at all, so a balance between both is important.

2. **Provide guidance in balancing adaptations.** Guskey writes (p. 57), "When innovations are implemented, change takes place in two directions. Individuals must adapt in order to implement new policies and practices. . . . The innovation also must be adapted to fit the unique characteristics of the context."

3. **Offer feedback to confirm that the change makes a difference for students.** Guskey writes that teachers need to

receive frequent and specific feedback on results. They need to know that what they are doing is working.

4. **Ensure that the feedback is based on evidence that teachers trust.** This is a point from Guskey that I have used in other books. Teachers typically will trust evidence that comes from classroom observations and classroom assessments, while school leaders tend to trust nationally normed or state assessments. It's important for teachers and leaders to have a dialogue about the type of evidence that needs to be collected and that both parties will find valuable.

5. **Plan to gather evidence on effects quickly.** Guskey raises the point that teachers will need evidence rather quickly on whether what they are doing is working or not. If they have to wait months for feedback or evidence that something is working, they may abandon it far too soon and go back to the practices they feel comfortable with.

6. **Provide ongoing support . . . with pressure.** We know that learning, especially involving students, is not always a smooth process. There are days when we take one step forward and the next day, we take two steps back. Guskey says that ongoing support and the pressure to keep moving forward is key.

Guskey's research on effective professional learning and development is key in our conversation about strengthening our ILTs as well as the joint work they engage in with staff and teachers in their school. Asking teacher leaders on the team to take leadership positions or engage deeply in new conversations with their colleagues at professional learning community (PLC) meetings or in staff meetings is not easy, and some of Guskey's suggestions are key for that process.

However, the professional learning and development those teacher leaders provide to the staff and other teachers in their school need the same considerations. When we think about the chapters on well-being, context beliefs, and workload, we know that professional learning and development can either alleviate the stress that comes with those three drivers or it can compound it. Teams need to make sure that they are clear on the outcomes they want, have included teacher and student voice in the process, and set out ongoing professional learning and development as well as the support needed in order to meet those outcomes.

NOTES

LEADERSHIP DEVELOPMENT

As ILTs learn and grow together, members of the team need to learn what it means to be part of a functional and impactful team. We have to remember that most members of an ILT, such as instructional coaches, teacher leaders, or union representatives, do not necessarily have leadership experience. Understanding how to implement improvement, facilitate faculty meetings around improvements, be a lone voice among a grade-level team to advocate for the improvement, and have a voice in the process with the team does not come naturally to everyone. Many teachers are used to being on teams but not having a voice; they are used to a top-down model. Professional learning and development is important to the team improvement process.

Campbell et al. (2017, p. 8) found that there needs to be a flip "from top-down governance to a system where teachers have opportunities to exercise collective autonomy, professional judgment, and leadership of educational change." This shift away from top-down authority to collective autonomy will help school leaders adopt a learning mindset; it shows them that they do not always have to lead alone. This ability to flip the hierarchy is the reason why I included mindset as a driver to building collective leader efficacy.

The Department of Education of Western Australia (2018, p. 3) writes,

> Gone are the days when leaders could make a decision and expect it would be unquestioned and acted on because of the authority of the principal. Environmental mindfulness, interpersonal and communications skills assume a higher profile in this climate.

Harris (2013, p. 551) writes,

> One thing is absolutely clear: formal leaders acting alone will not achieve school and system transformation. Meeting the educational needs of the 21st century will require greater leadership capability and capacity than ever before within, between, and across schools. It will demand that formal leaders concentrate their efforts on developing the leadership capability and capacity of others, both in their school and other schools.

This will be a shift in mindset for many school building leaders, and this intersects greatly with our chapter on working conditions. For positive working conditions to be fostered, there needs to be an increase in the joint work that teachers can engage in with one another as well as the joint work that an ILT can do together, which means that school leaders need to know the difference between when to speak and when to listen, when to control and when to give up control. Professional learning and development is necessary to break school building leaders out of a mindset of top-down decision-making and turn toward a more collaborative decision-making process, which will dramatically improve working conditions for everyone.

The Department of Education of Western Australia (2018, p. 7) writes, "The core of a school leader's job is to create the conditions under which every teacher can perform at their maximum effectiveness." This means that leaders leave behind the need to go it alone and focus on the need to engage in authentic work with others.

As you may imagine, abandoning the need to go it alone and make decisions in isolation can be difficult for school building leaders because they feel so much pressure to have all of the answers when others are coming to them with questions. COVID was highly stressful because school building leaders wanted to have all of the answers and put the pressure on themselves to do so, but the climate changed drastically due to COVID cases and contact tracing; the answers had to come from the group and not only from one individual.

INDIVIDUALS NEED TO GROW AS LEADERS

As I wrote earlier, professional learning and development in the case of ILTs is not only about the actual school building leader, it is also about allowing and encouraging others to step up to take on leadership roles. In research, this has often been referred to as *distributed leadership*. Harris (2013, p. 548) writes,

> Simply advocating distributed leadership without adequate consideration of exactly what is being distributed is much more than a matter of ideological point scoring, it has real implications for those working in schools. It is whether and how distributed leadership influences organisational performance that matters most of all.

This is why, in several places in the book, I have advocated for a variety of roles on the ILT. Those roles will help individuals on the team to step up to a leadership role they may find uncomfortable. Those roles may provide a stepping stone to other leadership positions within the team. Harris (2013, p. 551) goes on to write,

> Distributed leadership is not simply about creating more leaders. The steady accumulation of more and more leaders does not equate with distributed leadership. The issue is not one of increasing the numbers of leaders, but rather one of increasing leadership quality and capability.

"The issue is not one of increasing the numbers of leaders, but rather one of increasing leadership quality and capability."

What we know from research focusing on assistant principals is that many assistants have only been allowed to do master scheduling and student discipline, giving them very little time to devote toward team building and instructional leadership; although the tasks have been distributed, it does not necessarily mean that there is a positive impact on student learning.

As we also learned in this book, instructional coaches and teacher leaders need to be prepared for taking on leadership roles because many of them have not gone to university for a leadership degree and never received the pre-service leadership professional learning and development that school building leaders and assistant principals received, yet they are put into a leadership position. The fact is that teacher leaders and instructional coaches who are on ILTs need professional learning and development to help foster the leader within, which also means they need to know how to share that power collectively.

To further support the research from the Department of Education in Western Australia, and in an effort to provide an example of how power is shared, I am providing a vignette written by Western Australia principal, Raymond Boyd.

WORKING COLLECTIVELY, NOT JUST COOPERATIVELY

West Beechboro Primary School (WBPS) is a Level 5 public school located in Perth, Western Australia (WA). The school currently has 500 students from kindergarten (4-year-olds) through to Year 6 (12-year-olds). Since I was appointed to the school in 2006 (and then subsequently winning the permanent position at the school in 2008), the school's teaching and learning community has undergone significant change that has resulted in our student population achieving at high levels for many years. This has not occurred serendipitously but rather was the result of deliberate and purposeful leadership.

Starting off, the small leadership group included, primarily, one deputy principal. The leadership team was expanded over time to include teacher leaders who not only shared the belief that our students were capable of so much more but who had demonstrated through their classroom practices that they were able to help students reach beyond their own expectations.

Since 2010, there has been a significant shift in the overall decision-making processes, in particular in the concept of *consensus* within the school. I saw the concept of *consensus* as a contentious one in that there would always be individuals or groups of individuals who did not support a particular change simply due to the fact that it may mean being uncomfortable in making the change either through a lack of knowledge or understanding or because they simply desired to maintain the status quo.

Further contentiousness exists within the school paradigm because, despite the system promoting collaboration, consensus, and shared decision-making and the need to move away from top-down decision-making, the end line accountability rests entirely with the principal, and this was something I stressed to my leadership team.

In an effort to work within this paradigm (while at the same time, work around it), we introduced three phase teams across the school:

- Junior phase (Kindergarten to Year 2)

- Middle phase (Year 3 to Year 4)

- Senior phase (Year 5 to Year 6)

With the finalization of the school plan, the school's leadership group saw a unique opportunity to redefine what we did as leaders in the school to contribute to this vision. This was a chance to ensure that, like the growth of the school, we, too, had current educational research relative to what defines a highly effective school and how leadership could contribute to that.

To do this, we ensured that professional development was closely aligned with effective curriculum delivery. Our leadership team continued to develop and clearly outline an instructional delivery framework that ensured the highest levels of consistency, both within year levels and across year levels, to enable seamless transitions from year to year. We did this by using an effective teaching model (ETM) for consistency across all classrooms. The team saw this as being vital to our ongoing improvement as a teaching professional at WBPS and that we had a commitment to the identified pedagogy within the school, to our students, to each other, and to the leadership team; this was where the phase teams and phase leaders played a significant role.

Professional Learning and Development

Each phase is directed by an identified lead teacher. This is a classroom teacher who is an expert in classroom instruction within that phase. These teachers had already established credibility with their colleagues and could walk the walk and talk the talk in terms of being in the thick of instruction. The phase leaders operated within specific, collectively agreed-on terms of references, with their role including

(Continued)

(Continued)

- running demonstration lessons,
- observing teaching and learning,
- providing direction for improvement and
- encouraging and modeling professional reflection.

Each fortnight, the phase teams would meet in their own clusters to set goals for the phase and celebrate the success of individual teachers in terms of innovative and progressive pedagogy in relation to the improvement of student outcomes. In this way, and through this structure, teachers were held accountable to the decisions and processes put in place by the phase and they were part of these decisions. Staff still had a degree of autonomy within their classroom in the form of a connected autonomy, ensuring consistency of curriculum content, content delivery, and structural processes.

Instructional alignment is something we have worked toward for many years at WBPS. It forms a small but important part of whole school alignment. At WBPS, we have coached staff to an established ETM, which has become our instructional framework or, for a better description, our signature pedagogy.

During morning walk-throughs and informal observations, it becomes clearly evident that we have achieved instructional alignment across the school's teaching and learning community. Clear evidence of common planning tasks and obvious similarities in lesson structure indicate that coaching in our ETM is having and has had an impact. When walking through the classrooms each morning, I see the collective positive impact that this instructional alignment has had on both staff and students.

This has been due in no small part to the work of the school's leadership group and the collective efficacy that they have around student improvement and teacher practice, with many members of the school leadership team also stepping into the teacher's role to run a demonstration lesson for the classroom teacher. This often-overlooked role of the school leader helps to build currency or retain credibility with the teaching staff.

Over the years, my focus has remained on what happened in every room of the school because, as Dinham, Ingvarson, and Kleinhenz (2008) stated, "The major challenge in improving teaching lies not so much in identifying and describing quality teaching, but in developing structures and approaches that ensure widespread use of successful teaching practices: to make best practice, common practice." Chance is not something that a students' educational success should be based on; for this reason, I worked to ensure that our instructional rounds, observational practices, and coaching all centered on improving teachers' instructional capacities.

Efficacy at Work

A teacher's belief in their own self-efficacy, as has been noted in research, influences the extent to which teachers feel they are effective. This has been shown to influence subsequent teaching practices and pedagogical approaches. Teachers with high self-efficacy tend to engage more frequently in behaviors correlated with high pupil achievement than do teachers who possess low self-efficacy. For this reason, my senior administration team continues to revisit our school's programs to ensure that all staff are knowledgeable not only in content but also, more importantly, in curriculum delivery. Their knowledge and understanding can influence what teachers do in the classroom. The role of the phase teams is a pivotal point in this equation.

I have recently exposed the school's teaching community to the WA Future Leaders Framework, a program that was developed by the WA Department of Education's Leadership Institute and is targeted at identifying, developing, and supporting high-potential leaders within schools. For our team, this will provide a more formalized structure to how leadership is developed across the school, starting with the leadership of self and progressing through emergent leadership, team leadership, and school leadership. I will be able to strengthen the understanding of the impact that collective leadership efficacy has on student achievement and school improvement even further.

—Raymond Boyd
Principal
West Beechboro Primary School
Perth, Australia

What Boyd was able to do in his school—and continues to do to this day—is heavily supported by research.

Harris (2013, p. 551) writes,

> The core task of the formal leader is to support those with the expertise to lead, wherever they reside within the organisation. It is to judge when this expertise is needed for the development

of the organisation and to engage this expertise in an authentic and respectful way. The main challenge for formal leaders who want better performance and better outcomes is to actively build the leadership capacity within their organisation, so that productive change and continuous improvement can become a real possibility.

This takes work; sometimes it begins with how we develop the work together and then how we promote it to the rest of the school community. There should always be time set aside within the ILT not only to talk about the resistance that may be taking place in the school around an initiative but also to have a conversation about ways to address the resistance. Additionally, every time that members of the team are asked to take information back to their colleagues, there should be conversations among the team about the best ways to deliver those messages. We will address this further in Chapter 8 by focusing on the skills to work in collectives.

As I close out this section on leadership professional learning and development, I want to offer some suggestions on areas that ILTs can focus on in their internal professional learning and development.

WHERE SOURCES OF EFFICACY INTERSECT WITH PROFESSIONAL LEARNING AND DEVELOPMENT

Master Experience

- **Cycle of inquiry.** I know I have mentioned this a few times before, and it will certainly be our focus in Section III, but cycles of inquiry provide us with a great opportunity to engage in impactful professional learning and development.

Vicarious Experience

- **Flip meetings.** Provide information ahead of meetings. One of the reasons why individuals on a team do not feel comfortable speaking about a topic is that they do not feel confident enough. In other words, they lack self-efficacy. Sending an article, blog, or video in advance of a meeting is a good way to provide information and help people feel informed so that they will have confidence when speaking during the meeting. I like to provide three questions I'm thinking about after reading the article and ask people to develop three of their own so we can discuss them together.

Verbal Persuasion

- **Common language/common understanding.** Develop a common language and common understanding on your team for topics such as student engagement, feedback, or de-implementation. What do these words mean in your school? A common language and common understanding bring clarity, which helps greatly when it comes to how we communicate with one another.

- **Protocols.** Engage in protocols to ensure that everyone around the table has the opportunity to share their voice in some capacity and that no one person is monopolizing the conversation. Make sure protocols focus on social sensitivity (you will learn more about this in Chapter 8) so each member of the team feels valued, even if their message is not as loud or strong as others around the table. Encourage the use of protocols at all meetings and not only those of the ILT.

Affective States

- **Agency among teachers.** Take time to engage as an ILT around how teacher leaders can go back to their constituency and talk about the decisions the team made together. In Chapter 7, you will learn about the collective responsibility of the team. Each member has a collective responsibility to share their voice in the process and support the process when decisions are made.

STUDENT COUNCIL REFLECTION

How can ILTs ensure that student councils are learning how to collaborate and lead? It is so important for their development as adolescents and a team to learn from one another and to guide learning as well. How might this look? Does every member of the student council have a particular function and job role? At that age, there can be individuals who want to take on a majority of the work; however, what's important is learning how to collaborate as a team.

Professional learning and development is always a hot topic. As someone who facilitates workshops but was also a school principal during a period of time when there was great accountability, professional learning and development is important because schools are meant to be learning organizations. However, learning doesn't always happen in compliance and many schools are under deep compliance measures.

I was in the same predicament of accountability when I began flipping our faculty meetings and focusing on learning. Just like I had to do back then, we need to reflect on how we engage in professional learning and development, learn from it, and decide where to go next.

This whole topic coincides with our focus throughout the book on de-implementation, because we need to decide what practices should be fostered and which practices should be let go. What this means is that we have to decide what professional learning and development should be abandoned. I believe one-day sit-and-get workshops should be traded in for longer, more consistent inquiry-based professional learning and development so that we can create a community of learners around topics that will help us impact student learning the most.

In order to do that, I'd like you to take some time to reflect on your current professional learning and development by using the SWOT analysis in Activity 6.1 below.

Activity 6.1
SWOT Analysis
Your Professional Learning and Development

To gain a better understanding of your current reality when it comes to professional learning and development, try another SWOT analysis. Take some time with your team to focus on your current reality when it comes to how you offer professional learning and development. If your professional learning and development is not effective, how will you rectify that using the information from this chapter?

Professional Learning and Development: SWOT Analysis

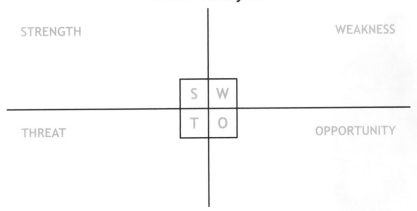

IN THE END

This chapter on professional learning and development explored three issues: (1) clarifying what constitutes professional learning and development, (2) examining how the ILT and student council engage in professional learning and development, and (3) asking how the team takes elements of effective professional learning and development and uses them to offer learning to staff that will be impactful and focused on outcomes. Joint work is a key aspect of effective professional learning and development, and it should certainly be a key element to strengthening the ILT.

GUIDING QUESTIONS

- What is the difference between professional learning and professional development?

- What professional learning and development is needed for each individual on the team to be successful?

- What is the necessary professional learning and development your instructional leadership team needs to successfully have an impact on student learning?

(Continued)

(Continued)

What two questions do you wish I had asked?

1.

2.

What three new areas of learning did you experience while reading this chapter?

1.

2.

3.

NOTES

ORGANIZATIONAL COMMITMENT

7

Although people often talk about ... commitment in general terms, it is important to specify "commitment to what?"

William Firestone and Sheila Rosenblum (1988, p. 287)

THEORY OF ACTION

If . . . an organization commits to improving the learning environment of their students, then . . . their students will experience a much more impactful learning environment.

GUIDING QUESTIONS

- In what ways do you feel that your organization is committed to you?
- In what ways are you committed to your organization?
- Why is organizational commitment sometimes complicated?
- What is your team's organizational commitment when it comes to student learning and the school's instructional core?
- How does an understanding of organizational commitment contribute to strengthening your instructional leadership team?

The theory of action that I wrote at the beginning of this chapter sounds like common sense. I wanted to write what I was thinking in a positive way because what I was truly thinking is, "If an organization doesn't know what it is committed to, then they will never commit to anything."

Organizational commitment can be interpreted in a few different ways. Organizational commitment is often seen as feelings of achievement that people experience when doing their work every day and how dedicated or loyal an individual is to an organization (which, for our purposes, is a school; Morrow, 1993). Mowday et al. (1979, p. 604) defined *organizational commitment* as "the relative strength of an individual's identification with and involvement in a particular organization."

For our purposes, organizational commitment can include our commitment to our school district or ministry of education or, quite simply, our commitment to our individual schools. It is important to remember that in typical school districts around the world that have multiple primary, middle, and secondary schools within their jurisdiction, organizational commitment can mean how teachers are committed to their schools and their districts and how those in a district office are committed to their schools, teachers, and students.

Research shows that a teacher's organizational commitment is directly impacted by school organizational factors, such as school leadership (Hoy et al., 1990; Hulpia et al., 2011; Koh et al., 1995; Nguni et al., 2006). One of the interesting aspects of the early research on a school leader's impact on the organizational commitment of teachers is that it focuses on leadership being about one person—one school building leader. What we know now is that distributed leadership is more about how leaders work with teachers and staff as well as how they inspire and motivate others to lead. When it comes to distributed leadership, Spillane et al. (2001) explain,

> We are specifically concerned with developing a distributed leadership framework for thinking about leadership as practice as it relates to the transformation of teaching and learning. By taking leadership practice in a school as the unit of analysis, rather than an individual leader, our distributed theory of leadership focuses on how leadership practice is distributed among both positional and informal leaders. (p. 24)

Distributed leadership, when done well through the use of providing job roles as we laid out earlier or understanding drivers before or during the engagement of the work an instructional leadership team

(ILT) does, can contribute to a sense of organizational commitment because people feel that they are giving to the greater good and they see that their organization appreciates their contribution.

ILTs, the focus of our instructional core, and the process of building collective leader efficacy are the closest most leaders can come to distributed leadership while taking responsibility for the whole school.

Commitment on the part of teachers and leaders to an organization should not be one-sided. It is not only about how committed a teacher or school building leader is to a school; it is also about how dedicated a school system is to supporting the needs of teachers and leaders. This is a good place to pause and reflect on how a student council fits into this equation.

STUDENT COUNCIL REFLECTION

As we are learning in this chapter, organizational commitment is a two-way street. If your school community has a student council, how is your organization committed to them? Does your student council feel that their voices are valued?

As I stated earlier, when we get to Section III, you may consider having your student council (if one exists in your school) engage in a cycle of inquiry to help deepen learning in your school. In order to do that, the student council members need to feel valued.

Lastly, what actions does the student council take to improve your organization?

One of the first drivers I suggested for building collective leader efficacy is context beliefs. Do teachers and leaders believe that their school system will support them if they try innovative practices? If teachers and leaders do not hold those context beliefs, then it will be difficult to get organizational commitment from those teachers. The methods in which to do that are what this book is all about. Teachers' and leaders' mindset, voice, agency, and understanding of the drivers necessary to build a more impactful ILT are what is needed to enhance the organizational commitment people feel to a school.

Alone, with a partner, or with your team, consider these reflection prompts regarding organizational commitment. This activity is focused on the drivers of context beliefs, organizational commitment, and mindset.

REFLECT

List three ways you believe your organization (school or district) is committed to you:

1.

2.

3.

List three ways that you are committed to your organization (school or district):

1.

2.

3.

List three ways those commitments impact students in positive ways:

1.

2.

3.

WHY IS ORGANIZATIONAL COMMITMENT IMPORTANT?

Organizational commitment is important to student achievement. Firestone and Pennell (1993) write,

> What teachers are committed to can make a difference. A commitment to students may contribute to a warm, supportive climate that is likely to reduce the dropout rate but may not contribute much to academic achievement, while a commitment to teaching may have the opposite effect. (p. 491)

This is often a very difficult discussion because it brings about the need for balance between the empathy and empowerment we have to foster with students and the push toward higher academic growth. As a former primary school teacher and principal, I found myself in the middle of discussions that often involved the words *poor baby* because teachers felt bad about the home life of the student; those students may live in poverty or in a one-parent household. Sometimes *poor baby* meant that the student struggled academically and the teacher was concerned that the student would struggle throughout life, which is something we don't know will happen and we have no control over. Our job is to empower students, not enable them.

Although it is highly important to consider the home life of children, we have to be careful not to enable them instead of empowering them. The "poor baby" syndrome can actually create a deficit thinking on the part of adults because they view the child through a sympathetic lens that may actually prevent those same adults from seeing that the child needs to be empowered to learn. Empowering them to learn may help students get out of their circumstances, but deficit thinking and too much sympathy on the part of teachers toward the student may never help that student get out of their circumstances. We, as teachers, need to be committed to both.

Low teacher commitment can have a negative impact on student learning. Firestone and Pennell (1993, p. 493) write, "Low teacher commitment also reduces student achievement. Burned-out teachers are less sympathetic toward students, have a lower tolerance for frustration in the classroom, and feel more anxious and exhausted."

As you can understand, all of the chapters leading up to this can help engage teachers and staff in dialogue around social-emotional and academic learning, which will also help build organizational commitment. Although we now understand the importance of commitment, we should turn our focus to what we should be committed to as an organization.

WHAT SHOULD YOUR TEAM BE COMMITTED TO?

We know from this book that student learning is the greatest commitment, and in Chapter 10, we will dive deeper into your instructional core and what that means. For now, I'd like you to think about all of the aspects of student learning in your school, and consider which ones are the most important. These are the aspects that you should be committed to the most.

Think of it this way. If we were visitors walking into our schools with a nonjudgmental mindset and asked random teachers, students, staff, and parents what our school was committed to, what would their answers be? I feel as though school leaders and teachers are so busy surviving during these stressful times of testing, accountability, mental health issues, and the whole host of other issues that schools face each year that they need to be intentional about what they are committed to as a school. Firestone and Rosenblum (1988, p. 287) write, "Although people often talk about . . . commitment in general terms, it is important to specify 'commitment to what?'" I understand that these are big questions, and people often think these are questions that researchers and authors care about, but given the issues of race, equity, and political divisiveness that go on in so many countries around the world, it is a topic that should be important for every school, too.

When you think about your own organization, what are you committed to? I'd like you to do some work in Activity 7.1 with your partner or team and write down the goals you have when it comes to student learning.

Activity 7.1 Which Goals Are You Really Committed to?

As a group, reflect on the needs of your school. Take some time to create a list of ten issues around learning that your group is committed to.

1.

2.

3.

4.

5.

6.

7.

8.

9.

10.

(Continued)

(Continued)

If you have learned anything in this book, it's that we have too many initiatives and too many areas of focus. Take your list of ten and reduce it to five.

1.

2.

3.

4.

5.

How was the conversation? Was it easy to break your list down to five or was it difficult? Now, I would like you to break it down to three.

1.

2.

3.

Is your organization really committed to meeting these final three needs? Would you prefer that your organization be committed to three different needs (not identified here)?

 **NOTES**

I'd like to test your list of three issues that your school is committed to. During the COVID pandemic, I began moderating a web show called A Seat at the Table for *Education Week*. My editor Elizabeth Rich and I wanted to focus on topics of race, equity, grading, mental health, ethics in leadership, and every topic we could think of under the umbrella of education. I interviewed experts such as Zaretta Hammond, John Hattie, Tom Guskey, Tyrone Howard and his son Jaleel Howard, Andre Perry, Andy Hargreaves, and Alison Skerrett as well as lesser-known school practitioners. As we focused on racism and equity, one topic kept coming up in every episode: deficit thinking.

Too often, we place different expectations on students of color; students from indigenous populations such as Native American, First Nations, and Aboriginal students; and students living in poverty. Those students are often lumped into the "poor baby" syndrome or worse, these students receive harsher discipline and are seen as students who cannot achieve as well as their white peers. Some of my guests on A

Seat at the Table actually said they have heard the surprise and shock in the voices of teachers when students of color and other marginalized students achieve high academic success.

In primarily white schools, students from the dominant group lack exposure to students from other races and cultures and begin developing implicit biases toward them based on images they see in the media or on television. What this means for a school's organizational commitment is that ILTs need to not only look at instructional strategies and student engagement, but they also need to look at how teacher and leader implicit biases may lead to a lack of student engagement. Fullan and Quinn (2016, p. 18) write, "Leaders must first understand their own moral purpose and be able to combine personal values, persistence, emotional intelligence, and resilience. This is essential because their moral purpose will be reflected in all their decisions and actions." I would like to extend that to the whole ILT in the following deliberate practice reflection.

ILTs will never go deeper in their impact on student learning if they do not have open discussions about their moral purpose and implicit biases. Perhaps this is an area in which one of the school team members takes the lead because they feel efficacious in this area.

Each one of these focus areas offers examples for ILTs to strengthen their organizational commitment to their instructional core. As we close out this chapter and begin to move into our last two drivers, discuss these necessary antecedents to building organizational commitment.

- ILTs are invested in supporting the implementation of high-leverage practices within their school.

- ILTs are invested in supporting the de-implementation of practices that provide no evidence of impact.

- ILTs collectively understand the needs of their building.

- ILTs are committed to supporting staff and students in learning pursuits.

- ILTs understand that one uncommitted person on the team can have a negative impact on the rest of the team (i.e., an assistant principal who doesn't meet with the group).

- ILTs collectively have the knowledge to create goals that will improve their school climate.

In lieu of offering examples of a breakdown of organizational commitment related to Bandura's four experiences, I want to be spontaneous here and offer a powerful vignette by Alison Mitchell and Madelaine Baker from Glasgow, Scotland. I have worked with leaders in Glasgow several times, so I know Alison and Madelaine well. Their work, and what they provide in the vignette are not only a prime example of organizational commitment, but the vignette is also a perfect example of the skills to work in collectives, which is the next chapter you will explore when it comes to drivers of collective leader efficacy.

AN ORGANIZATIONAL COMMITMENT TO CLOSING THE ATTAINMENT GAP

Alison Mitchell

Head Teacher (School Principal), Rosshall Academy, Glasgow City Council, Scotland; Head Teacher in Residence, University of Glasgow, School of Education, Scotland

Madelaine Baker

Senior Deputy Head Teacher, Rosshall Academy

Equity and excellence and *closing the poverty-related attainment gap* are key Scottish government aims for education, supported by additional funding to individual schools across Scotland. Schools, therefore, have the autonomy to allocate the funding as appropriate to their school context to deliver the Scottish government's aspirations.

Rosshall Academy is a comprehensive city secondary (ages 11-18) school in Glasgow City. It has 1,278 pupils and a diverse pupil population:

- 53% of pupils reside in the 20% most-deprived locations in Scotland

- 12% of pupils do not have English as their first language, with 41 languages spoken across our school population

- 30% of pupils have recorded additional support needs.

Our work is underpinned by principles of social justice, inclusion, and six core educational values (Figure 7.1). These values were shaped and developed by the school community as a core set of principles by which we wanted our staff and young people to be defined. The values should be visible and evident in our communication, our actions, and our interactions. We promote an ethos and culture

(Continued)

(Continued)

whereby everyone in our school community assumes collective responsibility for every aspect of school life and we consider it a privilege to contribute to the life chances of young people in our care.

Figure 7.1

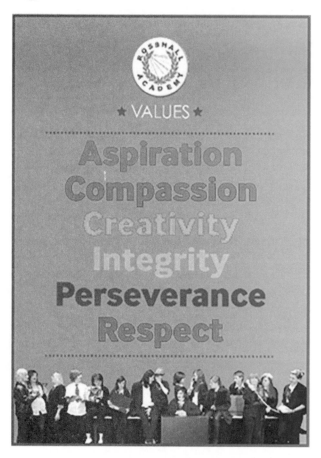

We expect that every member of staff will recognize their individual contribution and the difference they make not only to attainment or achievement in their specific subject areas but also to wider aspects of the school's success, such as the pupils' destinations, community well-being, the climate and ethos of the school, and our reputation.

We are embedding collective responsibility and social sensitivity—sensitivity toward the different groupings and roles within the staff, the status, and power relationships—through our staffing structure, our collaborative processes, our professional learning program, and our distributed leadership to ensure that all voices from across our community are heard and stakeholders feel trusted and valued. This vignette focuses on the leadership of our Middle Leadership Team (MLT) and our Teacher Learning Communities (TLCs).

Middle Leadership Team

While our staffing structure is, by the nature of the roles (head teacher, deputy head teacher, faculty head, principal teacher), hierarchical, there are strong horizontal connections within our MLT that promote social sensitivity through understanding and contribution to others' named remits to achieve our collective aims. This culture of collective responsibility is modeled by the senior leadership team, who all assume responsibility for every aspect of our school's work and support each other through the interconnectedness of each distinct remit. "Leadership development has a vital role to play in enabling leaders to have the required understandings, skills and stance for social justice leadership" (Forde & Torrance, 2017) and the revised professional standards for the teaching profession in Scotland articulate social justice as the responsibility of school leaders and teaching staff at all levels (General Teaching Council for Scotland, 2021).

Our MLT is currently the subject of a University of Glasgow School of Education research project examining social justice in middle leadership as part of a broader research project on the future of headship. Middle leadership roles have evolved in line with the changing nature of schools in a Scottish policy context that places equity and inclusion at its core. There can no longer be a longstanding separation between curriculum/subject leadership roles and pastoral care and welfare leadership roles. The interconnectedness and collaboration between the roles in our MLT—the trust, respect, and collective intelligence—serves the school community well. We were selected for this research because of the strength in our instructional core, with an extended leadership team that assumes collective responsibility, underpinned by principles of social justice, for contributing to the wider vision, aims, and aspirations of the school community.

1. We have an agreed-upon set of social justice-informed principles of mindsets (inspired by Datnow & Park, 2018) of inclusion (Figure 7.2) that underpin our practice, shaping our decisions about curriculum, learning and teaching, and our behavior, actions, and interactions. This ensures that our offer to our community is pupil centered to meet the individual needs and aspirations of every young person served by the school.

(Continued)

(Continued)

Figure 7.2 Inclusion Principles

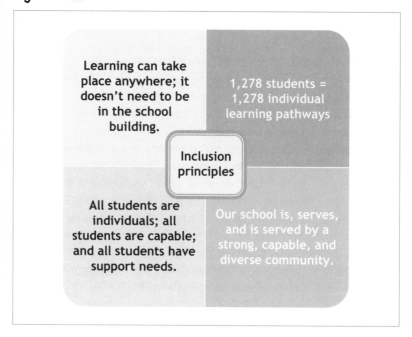

2. We recognize the interdependence of middle leadership roles and responsibilities in the areas of pastoral, curriculum, and equity issues. We nurture confidence and the skills in communication and collaboration to build collective intelligence and individual and collective efficacy.

3. We have made innovative use of the additional government funding in posts that reach out to isolated or underrepresented groups (e.g., our principal teacher of linguistic and cultural inclusion, our campus police officer, and our community learning officer).

4. We maximize the individual and collective impact of our middle leaders through promoting trust and collaboration not only between the MLT horizontally but across the vertical connections between the MLT and the senior leadership team and the MLT and the classroom teachers and support staff they lead.

It is important that leaders in our MLT present a collective, confident voice and promote the school values and principles of social justice. They should, in their leadership of staff, build the sense of collective accountability and thereby engage and motivate our staff to participate in all aspects of school improvement. We have further nurtured the collective confident voice in our teaching staff through the development of our TLCs.

Collective intelligence and collective accountability were the base concepts when developing TLCs in our school. At the fore was the importance of group composition and social sensitivities regarding roles, status, and contributions. Despite efforts to increase interdisciplinary learning, the Scottish secondary curriculum and assessment program, rather than focusing on the foundations of learning and teaching, remains predominantly subject based. Consequently, staff will often opt to work within their departments and resist working with other subjects. Therefore, bringing together teachers from different areas was critical in building collective efficacy. To ensure an understanding of the impact of TLCs, we reflected on Hattie's (2014) *Influences on Student Achievement*, which highlights the significant impact of collective efficacy.

We also considered the social aspect of the group composition. We had to meet staff where they were (DeWitt, 2016), acknowledging the "experience, assumptions and beliefs that participants bring to the collaborative activity" and the "circumstantial characteristics that define the levels of motivation, trust, symbiosis and synergy between individuals involved in the collaboration" (Mitchell, 2019, p. 58). We also had to be aware of the social sensitivities and varying levels of confidence in terms of contributing to the collective response.

Group composition (Figure 7.3) had to ensure a broad range of skills, subjects, personalities, knowledge, and leadership experience.

Figure 7.3 Teacher Learning Community Composition

Teacher Learning Community	
Teacher 1. Making Thinking Visible (MTV) leader (trained)	Teacher 7. Principal teacher (pastoral care)
Teacher 2. MTV leader (trained)	Teacher 8. Moderation planning group member
Teacher 3. Unpromoted teacher	Teacher 9. Unpromoted teacher
Teacher 4. Probationer teacher	Teacher 10. End of career teacher
Teacher 5. Unpromoted teacher	Teacher 11. Principal teacher (faculty)
Teacher 6. Digital leader of learning	Teacher 12. Deputy head teacher

(Continued)

(Continued)

In order to shift the collective responsibility away from a top-down approach, we looked for staff to volunteer as TLC leaders. There was no requirement for these staff to hold promoted positions within the school, but we wanted the staff who took these leadership roles to be open to developing themselves and others and engaging with professional learning. Leaders were given time to discuss their roles amongst themselves and to come up with suggestions and questions around the focus and the purpose of the groups. We also spent time discussing how to lead conversations, how to work with staff who were at varying stages of understanding, and how to empower individuals and groups to make contributions that will impact the work of the school as a whole. As a result of this leadership development, many of the teachers who undertook a leadership role have since moved into a formal promoted post.

Building Collective Efficacy

Although the TLCs were originally based on a specific learning program—Making Thinking Visible (Ritchhart et al., 2011)—the real purpose of creating these teams was to develop a sense of collective responsibility leading to collective efficacy. Hargreaves and O'Connor's (2018a) tenets of collaborative professionalism synthesize characteristics of effective collaboration, not least of which is the notion of collective efficacy: "the belief that, together, we can make a difference to the students we teach, no matter what" (p. 4). The original TLC model did not lend itself to a sense of self-efficacy or collective efficacy; staff were given a prescribed program to follow but as we developed the groups and broadened the focus, staff were given shared responsibility in the wider areas of learning and teaching and digital learning. We sought views from participants on the school's approach to these areas and engendered trust and confidence that their collective response would positively influence school decisions, which in turn built a sense of ownership across the staff.

The development of TLCs has had a significant impact on teacher confidence and willingness to share ideas and challenge others beyond their subject areas. Professional dialogue has a renewed focus, which sees a collective, creative, and innovative approach to learning and teaching and a shared vision for social justice that defines us as a school.

IN THE END

Developing strong ILTs is not easy. We sometimes follow the example of a past building leader or ILT that was not effective, which results in the school community having low expectations for our team. This is why we need to understand how to develop working conditions that are inclusive, supportive, and unique to our own context at a given time.

Organizational commitment is key to moving forward as a team. In Section III, we will explore the process for moving forward as a team. The learning that your team can gain when diving into these conversations will be something you remember for a long time. Some of the most difficult conversations I had with our ILTs are the ones that had the most positive impact on me overall.

GUIDING QUESTIONS

- In what ways do you feel that your organization is committed to you?
- In what ways are you committed to your organization?
- Why is organizational commitment sometimes complicated?
- What is your team's organizational commitment when it comes to student learning and the school's instructional core?
- How does an understanding of organizational commitment contribute to strengthening your instructional leadership team?

What two questions do you wish I had asked?

1.

2.

What three new areas of learning did you experience while reading this chapter?

1.

2.

3.

NOTES

THE SKILLS TO WORK IN COLLECTIVES

I find that one of the best, but most difficult ways for me to learn is to drop my own defensiveness, at least temporarily, and to try to understand the way in which his experience seems and feels to the other person.

Carl Rogers (1954)

THEORY OF ACTION

If . . . we understand that working collectively doesn't mean always getting our own way but is about how we learn from one another and move on together, then . . . we will have greater potential to confront our greatest issues.

GUIDING QUESTIONS

- What is collective intelligence?
- What part does emotional intelligence play in the skills to work in collectives?
- Why is communication important? What does the acronym WOVEN have to do with it?
- What areas of communication does your instructional leadership team excel at? Which areas of communication does your team need to work on?
- How does your team foster collective responsibility?
- What does social sensitivity look like among your team? How is it respected?

DEVELOPING COLLECTIVE INTELLIGENCE

The last two drivers for collective leader efficacy, which will be explored in these last two chapters of Section II, are defined as the skills to work in collectives and the confidence to work in collectives (Hattie et al., 2021). This chapter will be slightly longer than Chapter 9 because I would like to provide some background for both chapters and then dive deeply into the skills to work in collectives within this chapter and the confidence to work in collectives in Chapter 9.

Having the skills and confidence to work in a collaborative group leads to collective intelligence. Woolley et al. (2015) define *collective intelligence* as

> the ability of a group to perform a wide variety of tasks." The researchers focus on "two influences on a group's collective intelligence: (a) group composition (e.g., the members' skills, diversity, and intelligence) and (b) group interaction (e.g., structures, processes, and norms). (p. 420)

As a former teacher and school principal, I didn't receive any formal training on what it was like to work with adults. Like most of us working in education, I learned those skills on the job. As a teacher, I wrongly assumed that everyone was similar to me and had a willingness to work with others and learn from them. Perhaps it was due to the years I spent as a struggling learner and the pride I had as a teacher, but I wanted to soak up every bit of learning I could when I was on some leadership teams.

What I found is that not everyone felt the same. There were people who wanted to get their way, and when they didn't get their way, they would complain to their grade-level peers that they never had a voice in the process. There were other members of the team who sat in silence and waited to be told what to do. These were people who were either not confident in their voice with colleagues or had learned over the years that their voice was not valued, so they simply showed up to the meeting without any intention of speaking. How sad is that? Going to a meeting with no intention to share ideas or learn any new ideas is truly a waste of time. Developing collective intelligence is not easy, which is why we focus here on skills and confidence.

What makes working in collectives frustrating is that some of the instructional leadership teams (ILTs) that we participated in were never about fostering our voices as a collective. We were merely used as window dressing to make it look as though the principal cared about the staff's collective voices, when they would really just leave the meetings and do what they wanted.

Our ILTs need to be different. The skills of working in collectives begin with the school building leader setting the working conditions necessary for teacher leaders, assistant principals, and everyone else on the team to feel valued. Donohoo (2017) found that there are four leadership practices that are highly effective in developing collective teacher efficacy. These same four can be used to begin developing the collective skills needed to contribute to collective leader efficacy. Those four successful leadership practices that Donohoo highlights include the following:

1. **Creating opportunities for meaningful collaboration.** "Structures and processes need to be in place for educators to come together to solve problems of practice collaboratively" (p. 37). ILTs provide the structure needed to build collective leader efficacy.

2. **Continuum of collegial relationships.** "Teachers need to be introduced to processes that support joint work and aid in addressing challenges related to learning, leading, and teaching" (p. 38). Members of an ILT need to foster these relationships in order to get to the deeper work.

3. **Empowering teachers.** "When formal leaders provide opportunities for shared leadership by affording others the power to make decisions, everyone benefits" (p. 39).

4. **Teacher involvement in decision-making.** "There are varying degrees of involvement in school decision-making. Simply inviting participation does not guarantee that teachers will feel empowered" (p. 40).

These four leadership practices that Donohoo presents are necessary to our conversation here on building the skills and confidence to work in collectives, and we need not look any further than 2020 to understand why this work can be difficult.

POLARIZED INDIVIDUALS ON COLLECTIVE TEAMS?

Many situations offered learning lessons to educators in the United States in 2020. Besides the COVID pandemic, we faced a presidential election and the murder of George Floyd and many other innocent Black men and women. We saw increased visibility of the Black Lives Matter movement and then saw lawn signs stating that Blue Lives Matter and All Lives Matter. It seemed then and still seems now that people chose sides like they choose their favorite baseball, football, or hockey teams.

Those situations highlighted the polarizing nature of our beliefs in and out of school. It would be impossible for our country to be so polarized and not have people with drastically diverse views on these highly charged issues share the same school buildings—and perhaps the same ILTs. Our ILTs are places where liberals, conservatives, and everyone in between share the same table but not the same ideas. That can play out in aggressive and passive-aggressive ways, and there is no better place to figure all of this out than in our schools.

How we work together in collectives has always been complicated, but in 2020, it became increasingly so with the use of social media, especially media outlets that cater to only those viewers who are in line with their thinking. No matter what side we are on, we all experience a level of truth decay. Kavanagh and Rich (2018) write, "There are four trends that characterize truth decay." Those four trends are

1. increasing disagreement about facts and analytical interpretations of facts and data;

2. a blurring of the line between opinion and fact;

3. the increasing relative volume, and resulting influence, of opinion and personal experience over fact;

4. declining trust in formerly respected sources of factual information. (pp. 10-11)

This issue of truth decay inhibits our ability to engage in deep conversations as a team and develop collective intelligence. And one of the biggest discussions ILTs need to engage in is how to prioritize fact over opinion. This is critical not only for the big issues of race and equity but also for the discussions around what works in the classroom when it comes to student engagement and instructional strategies. We can no longer rely solely on the opinion that our gut gives us; we must provide evidence to determine whether our techniques work or not. We may not always agree, and that is healthy, but we do need to set the stage for engaging in these tough conversations as a group.

In my work, I have partnered with the New Brunswick Teachers Association (NBTA) in Canada over the past several years. They are a wonderfully inclusive group of leaders and teachers spread out across the scenic province. During many conversations with them, Dianne Kay, Gina Dunnett, Jay Colpitts, and Wayne Annis introduced me to the concept of *intellectual safety*. Regardless of the topics that an ILT engages in, they must provide a space for intellectual safety or the team will never go deep into these much-needed topics.

Baba (2019, p. 29) writes, "Intellectual safety encourages respectful relationships, meaningful learning environments, and productive disagreement with the potential to extend beyond the classroom." Research suggests that there are three team leadership functions, which are direction setting, developing leadership capacity and managing its ability to problem-solve, and empowering team performance (Burke et al., 2006).

Our ILTs are not about merely showing up anymore; they're about deep conversations that will strengthen the instructional core of a school while understanding what individual members bring to the table and how they interact with others. These final two drivers (the skills and the confidence to work in a collective) take all of those complexities into consideration. This is a good time to pause and consider the students. How can a student council engage in these conversations?

STUDENT COUNCIL REFLECTION

Students need to engage in discussions about what takes place in their society, and they do this by developing the skills to work in collectives and building collective intelligence. How does your student council develop collective intelligence together?

Please feel free to take a moment here to write down some notes about collective intelligence and the focus of societal issues before moving into the research around skills to work in collectives.

WHAT ARE THE SKILLS TO WORK IN A COLLECTIVE?

Most of us who come from a teaching background are used to being in control of the classroom. That control didn't mean that we were authoritative, but it did mean that we took hours to create lesson plans for each week and controlled which groups we saw and which ones worked collaboratively without an adult. We controlled parent-teacher conferences by focusing on report cards that we filled out, giving grades that we calculated. It doesn't mean we are bad people because we held so much control, but it does mean that entering into a collective of other teachers and leaders is not always comfortable.

This isn't only about teachers, either. As school principals, we are used to having control over the direction of the school, approving or disapproving of spending on classroom materials, controlling the discipline of students, and having a great deal of status that comes with our position. School building leaders are in a place of positional power, and they also have to learn the skills to work in a collective because if they choose that top-down language one too many times in an instructional leadership meeting, the collective is at great risk of not being a collective at all. It has the risk of becoming a dictatorship. It begins with improving our conversations.

Instructional coaching researcher Jim Knight has written extensively about better conversations, and true collectives need to focus on engaging in better conversations if they are to develop as a team and foster collective leader efficacy. Knight (2016, p. 6) says that better conversations are where we "position the person we are speaking with as a full partner rather than an 'audience.'"

The skills we need to work in a collective include emotional intelligence, communication skills, social sensitivity, and the ability to contribute to collective responsibility. Within each one of these skills are specific pieces to keep in mind. Some of these will be commonsense while others may provide insight that members of an ILTs may have not thought about. The first and probably most important of the skills to work in a collective is communication skills.

EMOTIONAL INTELLIGENCE

If Bandura is correct that we learn in a social context and Robinson is correct that schools are a learning organization and therefore it is not only our job to create and foster learning opportunities for students but it is also our job to engage in learning as adults, then we have to understand how to better slow down the process, listen to one another, and develop our best solutions. This takes *emotional intelligence*, which is an understanding of how to reflect and evaluate our emotions and the emotions of others and then decide the best course of action for moving forward. The Institute for Health and Human Potential (2019) writes,

> It's a scientific fact that emotions precede thought. When emotions run high, they change the way our brains function . . . diminishing our cognitive abilities, decision-making powers, and even interpersonal skills. Understanding and managing our emotions (and the emotions of others) helps us to be more successful in both our personal and professional lives.

Goleman and Boyatzis (2017) write that there are four domains to emotional intelligence: self-awareness, self-management, social awareness, and relationship management. The authors go on to say that there are 12 competencies housed under those four domains.

Self-Awareness

- Emotional self-awareness

Self-Management

- Emotional self-control
- Adaptability
- Achievement orientation
- Positive outlook

Social Awareness

- Empathy
- Organizational awareness

Relationship Management

- Influence
- Coach and mentor
- Conflict management
- Teamwork
- Inspirational leadership

What we can take from this research on emotional intelligence is that working in collectives is a lot more complicated than just sitting together at a table and making decisions. This is the reason why I have been introducing your team to the eight drivers. In fact, this research on emotional intelligence intersects with the mindset and well-being drivers that I introduced you to earlier, Mindset and well-being are what fosters these first two domains of self-awareness and self-management.

The skills to work in collectives and the confidence to work in collectives intersect with social awareness and relationship management. Goleman and Boyatzis (2017) write, "Simply reviewing the 12 competencies in your mind can give you a sense of where you might need some development."

However, what I would like to do now is to take the research on emotional intelligence and clearly outline some actions we need to take when it comes to emotional intelligence and the skills to work in collectives. It begins with how we communicate.

COMMUNICATION SKILLS

As an ILT, it's important to think about how we communicate with the rest of the school and school community as well as how we communicate with one another because it contributes to the collective intelligence of the group. For full disclosure, I have had to practice at a few of these because I was not as skilled at them as I had originally thought.

Communication is hard. It takes verbal and nonverbal skills as well as many other nuances we don't often think about until the communication goes wrong. As a school principal, besides the schoolwide team we created together, I was responsible for two grade levels across the district as part of our contract: "Duties as assigned." I'm sure many of you have that same language in your contracts. We only met once a month and most of the teachers came from other schools, so they did not know me well. It took time to establish trust; I had to learn how to communicate with them and they certainly had to learn how to communicate with one another.

I list four ways to communicate here. These are definitely areas that I had to work on. The acronym for them is WOVE, which stands for written, oral, visual, and electronic (Kress & van Leeuwen, 2001). I add nonverbal communication to this model, creating the acronym WOVEN.

COMMUNICATION SKILLS YOU CAN DEVELOP AS A TEAM

Written Communication

There are many studies that go into detail about the need for proper grammar when communicating, and this is a skill each and every member of the ILT needs to possess. As school personnel, it's clearly important to make sure that our written communication is devoid of grammatical errors because although people make mistakes, it's problematic when a school is the one making the error. We don't want to end up as figures of ridicule on Facebook!

Another equally important component of written communication is how the ILT sends out written communication to teachers and staff regarding the decisions being made around their instructional core focus. I abide by the "Goldilocks Principle": Is it too long, too short, or just right? A newsletter or electronic communication that is too long will most likely not get read by many; communication that is too short may be missing important information. The length of the communication matters greatly.

As a blogger for over 10 years, I have learned that you can say a lot in fewer words than you may imagine. Communicating to staff could be a duty for someone on the ILT. Perhaps there are one or two members on the team that are gifted in this department, so they could communicate for the team. The other thing to remember is that each member is a representative of their constituents, so there should be written communication that goes back to that constituency as well.

Oral Communication

Considering how important distance or remote learning became for so many of us during the COVID pandemic, and the fact that some of you may remain in those situations for a variety of reasons, oral communication could come in the form of short videos. In 2021, I created a newsletter called *Collective Conversations*, and many times, instead of writing a few paragraphs as a welcome, I recorded a two-minute video instead.

Our words matter, so how we choose to talk with one another—both internally on the team and externally to those within the school community—can either build a bridge or build a wall. I have been on the receiving end of conversations in which people clearly wanted to build a wall and let me know that nothing I had to say was important to them. However, I have also been on the receiving end of far more conversations in which people made me feel that my voice mattered; they went out of their way to make me feel comfortable.

This is where Jim Knight's *Better Conversations* work is highly valuable. Knight (2016) has written extensively about the need for individuals to be curious by asking questions during conversations, trying to build emotional connections with colleagues in the collective, and fostering dialogue.

Whenever I approach a conversation with someone, I try to be nonjudgmental and to prevent myself from interrupting others when they are speaking. These are two key actions Knight has highlighted as important when it comes to oral communication. So, I ask you, when working with the ILT, do you really listen and try to engage in dialogue or are you merely giving the person time without really listening to them? Over the years, I have tried to incorporate more coaching dialogue, such as requesting, "Tell me more"; I always try to go into each conversation being open to learning and not with the attitude that I already know all of the answers.

Visual Communication

Visual communication is how we send out visuals about the work our team is doing. This is a position someone on the ILT can take. Perhaps they are gifted when it comes to visual representations, creating sketches or notes, or using some other visual software tool. One of the actions I took as a principal was flipping communication. I created short informational videos for staff and families to provide information about school initiatives—for example, new anti-bullying legislation, standards, or what school looks like from the vantage point of their children. It's possible for someone on the ILT to take this role because it's important to provide visual and electronic information to teachers, staff, and families that will provide helpful information. There are two questions that your ILT will need to think about: Who will communicate for the team? Who will respond if the communication gets pushback from a staff member?

Electronic Communication

We understand already that electronic communication includes emails, the use of social media, and how we flip communication. In an effort to answer someone quickly, we have all responded in a way that ultimately created more work for ourselves because of the tone that was read into it or because we didn't provide enough

(Continued)

(Continued)

information. The same can be said for how we interact internally as an ILT. Those internal conversations that take place through email as a means to continue a discussion from the meeting will happen, but it's important to always take a breath before answering an email, and if you don't have anything to add at that time to the internal electronic conversation, then don't respond at all.

When the ILT communicates to staff, it's a good idea to designate one or two people to communicate electronically for the team. It's also important to highlight some standards so that other people on the ILT do not chime in to a whole-school communication and blow the whole thing up.

One more important point about electronic communication: I have been at countless meetings with school leaders and teachers who are attached to their phones. Whether they really need to be that connected or it's merely a visual cue to let everyone else around them know how important they are, our use of phones these days is often rude, and teams may want to establish a rule that phones are off during meetings.

Nonverbal communication

One area not represented in the Kress and van Leeuwen WOVE model—but of equal importance—is nonverbal communication, which moves us from WOVE to WOVEN. We know body language can give away our thoughts in the blink of an eye. Our body language and facial expressions can stop a conversation as easily as our words. As a person who doesn't have a poker face, I have had to learn how to control some of my body language and facial expressions in an effort to not interrupt a person who is talking.

When working within our collectives, we need to pay attention to our body language and facial expressions, which takes skill and practice. We want to make sure we are providing people with the space to share their ideas without the risk of our body language and facial expressions shutting them down.

Communication is definitely an important part of collaboration, but there are other skills necessary to be a part of a collective group, such as social sensitivity. Before we go there, though, take some time to engage in a reflection here by using the notes section below. What are your thoughts about WOVEN?

NOTES

SOCIAL SENSITIVITY

One of the domains introduced by Goleman and Boyatzis (2017) is that of social awareness, and the competencies within that domain are empathy and organizational awareness. Many teams set aside time to develop protocols to help individuals on the team understand when to speak, and many times, when not to speak. These can help a team prioritize conversations and keep them focused as a group. Unfortunately, all the protocols in the world will not help if teams do not first understand empathy and organizational awareness. In earlier chapters, I introduced you to working conditions, organizational commitment, and context beliefs, which are meant to deepen your understanding of organizational awareness. However, one last facet of the skills to work in collectives includes having the skill to develop social sensitivity, which helps develop empathy for others in the group.

Social sensitivity is our ability to understand the perspectives of other adults within our group. Pickett et al. (2004, p. 1095) found that "individuals who are especially concerned with social connectedness—individuals high in the need to belong—would be particularly attentive to and accurate in decoding social cues." The ability to read the table can lead to an increased sense of belonging among the group because those individuals feel understood. That connectedness can create the ability to delve into difficult topics because people feel that it is safe psychologically to do so. Pickett et al. (2004) found that teams with high levels of social sensitivity tend to perform well when completing a variety of specific collaborative tasks. Pickett et al. go on to write that "social sensitivity can be a key component in predicting the performance of teams that carry out major projects" (p. 403).

What we need to do is take the WOVEN concept and bring it to the next level, which is how people pick up on those nonverbal cues. It's important to do this because how we interpret the conversation and body language going on around the table contributes to or inhibits our sense of belonging.

Regardless of whether we are talking about the parent-teacher association/organization, professional learning community, or ILT, the work is important, but the connections created within the group are equally important. Those connections create a sense of belonging, and we know that Maslow (1968) placed belonging just after safety needs and basic physiological needs. This is not some touchy-feely philosophy I have; it is based on research from social psychology. Think of it this way: The opposite end of belonging is when people feel excluded, and Pickett et al. (2004, p. 1095) found that the "literature concerning social exclusion makes clear that a lack of belonging has powerful negative consequences." That's what can make our collectives so complicated, and it's a reason to understand social sensitivity.

It's because of this that I suggest that developing social sensitivity among our ILT is the best way to begin to chip away at those polarizing perspectives and understand one another. Research shows that the workplace is best positioned to facilitate this type of polarizing discourse (Mutz & Mondak, 2006).

To build social sensitivity among the ILT, members need to unpack this topic together and discuss what it could look like among their team. The topic of social sensitivity can be explored during group work by using protocols or activities, but the following work of radio host Celeste Headlee (2015) is a good place for teams to start.

STRATEGIES FOR BETTER CONVERSATIONS

In her powerful Ted Talk with nearly 23 million views, radio talk show host Celeste Headlee provides 10 ways in which adults can have a much deeper conversation by taking social sensitivity into account. The following are 10 ways to have a better conversation:

1. Don't multitask. Put down your phones and be 100% present.

2. Don't pontificate. Limit how much you talk on and on and on.

3. Ask open-ended questions.

4. Go with the flow. If thoughts come into your mind during the conversation, let them go. If they are important enough, they will come back to you.

5. If you don't know, say you don't know.

6. Don't equate your experience with theirs.

7. Try not to repeat yourself. People tend to bring up the same point over and over again and it can be condescending.

8. Stay out of the weeds. Our conversations do not have to be as detailed as we make them.

9. Listen more. "If your mouth is open, you're not listening." Headlee quotes Steven Covey by saying, "Most of us don't listen with the intent of understanding. We listen with the intent to reply."

10. Be brief. Headlee has a great image for this one, but I won't give it away. Watch the video.

One of the best quotations from Headlee's talk is when she quotes Bill Nye the Science Guy by saying, "Everyone you will ever meet knows something you don't." As a team, take less than 15 minutes to watch the video because it is truly one of the best Ted Talks I have seen that focuses on communication.

What research shows is that the more socially sensitive the group, the deeper the work that the group can accomplish. Through deep communication and an understanding of social sensitivity, members of the ILT will feel an increased sense of responsibility to the group, which is the next aspect of the necessary skills needed to contribute to the group.

CONTRIBUTE TO COLLECTIVE RESPONSIBILITY

Hargreaves and Shirley (2012, p. 176) write that teachers and leaders need to have a "collective responsibility for all students and the improvement of teaching, rather than individual autonomy from any interference or imposed accountability that eliminates professional discretion." If we remember from the beginning of the book, Dimmock (2016) wrote, "to be a system leader, s(he) must contribute to the greater good of other schools beyond their own" (p. 63). The same is true for teacher leaders, assistant principals, and instructional coaches on the ILT. The purpose of strengthening the instructional core is not about their own individual preferences; it is about contributing to the greater good of the school. This takes collective responsibility.

Collective responsibility is not easily achieved because members of an ILT are at risk of avoiding accountability (Lencioni, 2002) to the very responsibility they should share together. Why does this happen? It's actually quite simple.

On any given ILT, such as the one you are on presently, there are teacher leaders from grade levels or departments, an instructional coach or two, assistant principals, and one or two representatives such as teacher aides and school psychologists. When decisions are made by the team, and especially if some of the members do not feel as though their voices were heard during the process, those individuals on the team have to go back to their groups to talk about the decisions made by the ILT.

If those individuals have not felt heard, they will not take collective responsibility for the actions of the team. They will go back to their constituents and tell them that the decision was really made by the school leader and that they didn't have much of a choice in the process.

As part of the driver of having skills to work in a collective, each member of that collective needs to do their part in sharing responsibility for the decisions of the ILT. Without collective responsibility, the team will not be as impactful as it can be and will certainly not be a model of collaboration for the rest of the school community.

Through the shared work and dialogue of the team, deeper communication, and social sensitivity, individuals can build the skills needed to be a part of the collective. As we end this discussion of skills to work in the collective, I wanted to offer a deliberate practice activity (Activity 8.1) that can foster the collective responsibility needed for the ILT.

 # Activity 8.1 Deliberate Practice, Collective Responsibility

At the end of each ILT meeting, do the following:

1. Take time to reflect on the goals of the meeting. Keeping the agenda focused on a few important short-term and long-term goals will help the team feel a sense of accomplishment.

2. Consider how people have contributed to the achievement of the goals.

3. Create a closure meeting checklist with questions asking whether each individual on the team has taken at least one of the following actions:

   ✓ been a part of the communication process

   ✓ created a sketch or note to capture the thoughts of the team

   ✓ helped developed deeper thinking around the idea

   ✓ been heard when they had reservations about the ideas

4. Take a few moments to talk about how individuals on the team can approach the goals addressed with their constituency. Remember, not everyone on the team has a leadership background; they may need help with talking points. It might even be a good idea for the team to review the challenges that different stakeholders in the building may have with the decisions being made.

5. Fully discuss the concerns of different stakeholder groups within the school building to make sure that the decisions made around the instructional core are sound.

As we close out this chapter on the skills to work in collectives, we need to understand where what has been written intersects with that of Bandura's (1997) four experiences, which I have done in most of the other chapters.

WHERE SOURCES OF EFFICACY INTERSECT WITH THE SKILLS TO WORK IN COLLECTIVES

Mastery Experiences

- **Skills to work in collectives.** When we develop the skills to work in collectives, as we engage in a cycle of inquiry, it will result in mastery experiences that we can take with us for the next time we work together. Collective experiences where we listen to each other, learn from one another, and then engage in actions that have a deeper impact on student learning are mastery experiences.

Vicarious Experiences

- **Joint work.** Donohoo's (2017) work mentions the ability of teachers to engage in joint work. The whole idea behind joint work is not only to have a deeper impact on learning but also to allow opportunities where adults can learn from one another. The reason why social sensitivity and communication are needed is that we know we are at risk of engaging in critical conversations in which there may be polarizing views and we need to engage in these conversations with a mindset of learning from one another, not merely being right in our argument.

Verbal Persuasion

- **Communication.** Earlier in this chapter, we focused on emotional intelligence and types of communication (i.e., written, oral, nonverbal, etc.). How we communicate to others is important because our words have the ability to lift people up or break them down. If we are to get the most effort from people, then we need to find a balance between our critical feedback and our understanding of the social sensitivity of delivering communication in the most effective way.

> **Affective States**
>
> ● **Collective responsibility.** When people understand that they are a valued member of the team and are a part of the collective responsibility of that team, their confidence will increase.

IN THE END

When focusing on the skills to work in collectives, it comes down to emotional intelligence and collective intelligence, which means we have to focus on the ways we communicate, the social sensitivity we possess and the social sensitivity of others around the table, and the ability to take on collective responsibility.

What we know is that the joint work we engage in as an ILT has the potential to have a positive impact on student learning, but there are many nuances that come with that joint work. Setting protocols for our team may be important to how we run a meeting, but without understanding the drivers I have laid out so far, those protocols will not be as helpful as they could be.

It takes skill to work in groups, regardless of whether the group includes students or adults. Developing these skills can lead to our last driver: the confidence to work in collectives.

GUIDING QUESTIONS

● What is collective intelligence?

● What part does emotional intelligence play in the skills to work in collectives?

● Why is communication important? What does the acronym WOVEN have to do with it?

● What areas of communication does your instructional leadership team excel at? Which areas of communication does your team need to work on?

● How does your team foster collective responsibility?

● What does social sensitivity look like among your team? How is it respected?

(Continued)

What two questions do you wish I had asked?

1.

2.

What three new areas of learning did you experience while reading this chapter?

1.

2.

3.

NOTES

THE CONFIDENCE TO WORK IN COLLECTIVES

9

Group functioning is the product of the interactive and coordinating dynamics of its members.

Albert Bandura (1997, p. 477)

THEORY OF ACTION

If . . . teams can develop the confidence to work with each other on student learning, then . . . they will be able to have a deeper impact on the learning that happens in and out of their school community.

GUIDING QUESTIONS

- What does social sensitivity look like among your team? How is it respected?

- Why have school leaders been left out of the collective efficacy research?

- What are the four experiences that Albert Bandura's research shows have the most profound impact on fostering confidence among individuals and the whole instructional leadership team?

- What are some methods that teams can use to help individuals feel more comfortable contributing to their collectives?

The last driver is the confidence to work in collectives. For full disclosure, everything we have learned in this book has led up to this final driver. Mindset, well-being, context beliefs, and the other drivers are meant to help develop the confidence of the individuals on the instructional leadership team (ILT) as well as the confidence of the ILT as a whole group. The Cambridge Dictionary (2021) defines *confidence* as "the quality of being certain of your abilities or of having trust in people, plans, or the future." Confidence can best be seen through the lens of self-efficacy. I have often believed that within schools, people aren't resistant because they always want to be; sometimes people are resistant because they lack a level of self-efficacy in the task they are being asked to do. Yes, there are resistant people who don't lack self-efficacy, but sometimes that resistance comes from being forced to do yet another initiative that they didn't have a voice in the process of selecting.

Bandura (1997) writes,

> Self-efficacy refers to beliefs in one's capabilities to organize and execute the courses of action required to produce given attainments. . . . Beliefs of personal efficacy constitute the key factor of human agency. If people believe they have no power to produce results, they will not attempt to make things happen." (p. 3)

We know from Chapter 1 that self-efficacy is context specific (Tschannen-Moran & Gareis, 2007) and that not everyone will feel efficacious when it comes to being a part of a collective group. It takes confidence to work in collectives. Consider it this way: Imagine a group of teacher leaders sitting around the table with their school building leader, assistant principals, and instructional coach. There are issues of status, and the concern over disagreeing with the ideas of your supervisor can be a blow to anyone's confidence when sitting in a collaborative group. Confidence needs to be built through the ILT process, which is where collective leader efficacy enters into the equation.

Goddard et al. (2004, p. 3) write,

> In the past two decades, researchers have found links between student achievement and three kinds of efficacy beliefs—the self-efficacy judgments of students . . ., teachers' beliefs in their own instructional efficacy . . ., and teachers' beliefs about the collective efficacy of their school.

Goddard et al. (2000, p. 480) write that collective teacher efficacy includes "the perceptions of teachers in a school that the efforts of the faculty as a whole will have a positive effect on students."

As a former school building leader, it concerns me that school building leaders are left out of the equation when all of the research we have learned so far says that leaders set the tone for the workplace; in order for distributed leadership to take place so that teachers feel they have a voice in the process, they need the support and influence of the school building leader. We need to stop leaving the school building leader out of the equation as if they are a barrier to improvement instead of a positive influence in it. And school building leaders need to step up to the plate and stop acting as if the classroom is no longer their domain, when most of us spent years in the classroom before we chose to move into school leadership.

Goddard et al. (2000) go on to write,

> Teachers do not feel equally efficacious for all teaching situations. Teacher efficacy is context specific. Teachers feel efficacious for teaching particular subjects to certain students in specific settings, and they can be expected to feel more or less efficacious under different circumstances. (p. 482)

If teachers do not feel efficacious in all areas of teaching, then it makes sense that they are not going to feel efficacious when it comes to their role on a school leadership team, where they are potentially making decisions for other teachers within their schools. Confidence must be built during that process.

HOW IS CONFIDENCE BUILT?

Bandura (1997, p. 79) writes, "Self-efficacy beliefs are constructed from four principal sources of information." As a review of what has been covered in the previous chapters of this book, those principal sources of information that help people develop the confidence to work in collectives are (1) mastery experiences, (2) vicarious experiences, (3) verbal persuasion and allied types of social influences, and (4) physiological and affective states. These four experiences, and all of the drivers I have introduced to you, help build the confidence needed to work in collectives.

Goddard et al. (2000) write that the same four experiences that are relevant to raising the efficacy of individual teachers are equally as relevant for positively impacting collective efficacy and for building the confidence of the individuals as well as the whole group.

Bandura (1997) writes that mastery experiences "are the most influential source of efficacy information because they provide the most authentic evidence of whether one can muster whatever it takes to succeed" (p. 80). Bandura goes on to write that "successes build a robust belief in one's personal efficacy. Failures undermine it, especially if failures occur before a sense of efficacy is firmly established." Whatever goal around the instructional core is chosen by the team, we must have the confidence to stay strong through the bumps in the road because until efficacy is built, the team's goal is at risk of failing.

We must have the confidence to stay strong through the bumps in the road because until efficacy is built, the team's goal is at risk of failing.

Bandura (1997, p. 86) writes, "Efficacy appraisals are partly influenced by vicarious experiences mediated through model attainments. So, modeling serves as another effective tool for promoting a sense of personal efficacy." In fact, modeling under the right circumstances can have a positive impact on the efficacy of a teacher or group. "Seeing or visualizing people similar to oneself perform successfully typically raises efficacy beliefs that they themselves possess the capabilities to master comparable activities" (p. 87).

What this means is that when the ILT gets into the work together, there will be times when different members of the group may be asked to carry out tasks. Those tasks might be things such as discussing the attainment of instructional core goals at faculty and staff meetings or being a part of a learning walk or walk-through, and this can be an uncomfortable space for some teacher leaders. Learning by watching their colleagues from the ILT carry out these same actions may build the confidence of teacher leaders and inspire them to take on the role at the next meeting.

Additionally, where modeling pertains to building confidence for someone on a team, we can use modeling when it comes to how two people may interact with one another on the team. For example, a shy teacher on the team may learn how to find their voice and speak up a bit more by watching someone with that level of confidence on the team. These experiences are written in order of importance in Bandura's work, meaning that challenging activities are the most profound when it comes to building efficacy, and vicarious experiences are the second most profound. The third activity that helps build confidence is verbal persuasion.

Earlier in this book, we focused on communication through using the acronym WOVEN (written, oral, visual, electronic, and nonverbal), so this idea that verbal persuasion is impactful should not be a surprise. Bandura (1997, p. 101) writes, "It is easier to sustain a sense of efficacy, especially when struggling with difficulties, if significant others express faith in one's capabilities than if they convey doubts."

If an ILT is meant to develop the skills of the individuals around the table to strengthen the collective work, they need to understand how important it is to provide critical feedback as well as to express faith in one another as well as the team. It is one of the reasons why the skill to contribute to collective responsibility was covered in the previous chapter. How we talk to one another in the collective is vitally important.

Verbal persuasion also incorporates how we provide and accept feedback. In Section III, when we focus on learning walks, it's important to understand how that process can inhibit or support the self-efficacy of all teachers within a school, not only the teacher leaders who are a part of the ILT.

The last experience that has an impact on self-efficacy and collective leader efficacy is physiological and affective states. Stress can inhibit the contributions of those on a team, and excitement can be a positive factor in the contributions of the team. When we are stressed, we are at risk of shutting down, and when we are excited, we feel the strength to move on.

Bandura (1997) found that

> people often read their physiological activation in stressful or taxing situations as signs of vulnerability to dysfunction. . . . Thus, the fourth major way of altering efficacy beliefs is to enhance physical status, reduce stress levels and negative emotional proclivities, and correct misinterpretations of bodily states. (p. 106)

One of the many reasons why I highlighted well-being as a driver is because of the fact that stress leads to burnout; too many teachers and leaders are feeling an increase in stress. As we know, negative arousal can inhibit the self-efficacy process and the collective leader process. The well-being practices we focused on will go a long way toward having a positive impact on the physiological and affective states of the individuals on the team as well as the whole ILT.

THE CONFIDENCE TO CONTRIBUTE IDEAS

The confidence to work in collectives means that teams must foster a climate in which people on the team feel confident to contribute their ideas to the collective. Confidence takes place when people feel they can share their opinions, offer feedback, or contribute an idea or strategy that they believe will deepen the learning of the group.

For full disclosure, this was not ever easy for me when I was a part of collectives. As a teacher, I didn't always feel that I had a true voice in the collective, but I also lacked confidence. When I was a student and teachers cold-called me, I stumbled and could never answer the questions. This is a good place to pause and reflect on how the student council members can develop this confidence.

STUDENT COUNCIL REFLECTION

If the student council will be involved in the inquiry process that we will engage in throughout Section III, then it is important that each member develops the confidence to contribute to their group and possibly the school community as a whole. This is a lifelong skill.

How does your school community develop that confidence within the student council?

I never let go of that fear of being cold-called when I was a teacher, so immediate responses were not my forte; I had to develop the confidence to work in teams, which also meant developing the confidence to contribute ideas. What I was good at was reflecting on the conversation and contributing after that, so there are a few strategies we can look at that will help others develop that same level of confidence when it comes to work in collectives and contribute their ideas.

Those strategies, which also happen to be included throughout this book, include the following:

> **Goals.** One of the many reasons your team will engage in a cycle of inquiry is due to the fact that when your team defines the improvement goal together, more members of your ILT will feel

confident in contributing. People can't contribute when the goal is unclear.

▶ **Protocols.** Sometimes we have people who have too much confidence when it comes to working in a collective and contributing their ideas. Protocols help alleviate that issue. For example, I often use the World Café model in which a large group is divided into several smaller groups. Each of those smaller groups has a table host and the job of the table host is to make sure that everyone in that smaller group contributes ideas. At the end of the smaller sessions, the table host shares the group's ideas with the larger group. The table host duty changes every time there is a new conversation.

▶ **Roles.** Developing the skills to contribute means rethinking what it means to contribute. This is where we can develop different roles on the team (see Chapter 1 of this book). It also means that we change our perspective from the idea that contributing only means talking at a meeting and expand it to consider that contributing can also mean creating visuals, running professional learning and development at faculty and staff meetings, creating the notes for the team, or doing the research around the goal that the team is focusing on, which will help strengthen the instructional core of the school.

▶ **Flip meetings.** A few days before each meeting send the ILT a short blog or article or view a video (such as Celeste Headlee's Ted Talk) before the meeting so they have some level of knowledge coming into the meeting. This becomes easier the more often teams meet because it means different members can share a resource that the whole group can view before the next meeting. Flipping meetings really helps with the issue of self-efficacy. What we have learned in previous chapters is that self-efficacy plays a part in our level of confidence and that self-efficacy is context specific. Flipping meetings and giving people space to read or view something on their own provides them with the time to develop some confidence so they can contribute. If you're anything like me, you find it nearly impossible to be handed a document and then immediately asked if you have any input.

▶ **Encourage errors.** Teachers and leaders talk to students about making errors and learning from them, but we don't often practice what we preach. As a school principal, I was always honest about my errors and how I learned from them. We need to model that more often.

> **Facilitate meetings differently.** Besides flipping meetings so that people can read ahead of time, one of the strategies that I use to build confidence among teams is to take that flipped learning and have members of the team engage in learning activities in smaller groups. During remote learning, this meant that I would often give people time in breakout rooms so they could discuss the learning and engage in the activity within a smaller group. Many people don't feel confident to speak when they are in a group of 10 or more people, but when they are divided into groups of three or four, their level of confidence rises.

When we can expand on how we approach our meetings (such as using a flipped model) or expand on what it means to contribute to the collective, then we can begin to develop the skills of the people around the table. We may actually find there are roles and ways to contribute that we never considered before. I'm asking you to consider the roles that individuals on the team can take on and think about roles that may help others contribute to the collective in creative ways.

IN THE END

The confidence to contribute to the collective is our last driver before we move on to the practice section of the book. As we also learned and probably knew beforehand, confidence is an important factor when it comes to building individual efficacy and collective leader efficacy. Bandura's (1997) seminal work is influential here, as you have probably guessed. His principal sources of information—(1) mastery experiences, (2) vicarious experiences, (3) verbal persuasion and allied types of social influences, and (4) physiological and affective states—were not only groundbreaking at the time, but they are also still highly influential in the world of education and psychology today. I have made the case throughout Section II that how the drivers that I cited from previous research and the drivers that I have found in my own research intersect with the four experiences developed by Bandura (1997).

Before we end this section, I would like you to go through a group reflection activity so you can gauge where your team is when it comes to the drivers of collective leader efficacy. The following is a reflection with a 5-point Likert scale; 1 indicates that your team still has work to do when it comes to the driver and 5 indicates that your team is doing very well when it comes to the driver.

Activity 9.1 Likert Scale

Driver	1	2	3	4	5	Notes
Mindset						
Well-Being						
Professional Learning and Development						
Working Conditions						
Organizational Commitment						
Context Beliefs						
Skills to Work in Collectives						
Confidence to Work in Collectives						

Please remember that the drivers offer important consideration for how your ILT should function together, but very few teams will be able to offer an answer of 5 in Activity 9.1. It is equally as important to remember that even though we will leave these drivers in Section II and move on to Section III, this doesn't mean your team is finished with them.

As you move to Section III, your team will focus on the work, which means developing a cycle of inquiry; these drivers still need to be fostered as you go through each and every conversation. In fact, you would do well to revisit these drivers after your team develops their cycle of inquiry so that each member of the ILT understands how these drivers fit into the greater theory of action that you will develop. Doing so will ensure that fewer people leave the cycle of inquiry feeling unheard.

Lastly, as we move on to the practice section of the book, please remember that the ILT process is not easy. Sometimes we pay for the sins of the past because teacher leaders, assistant principals, and others have been on teams that were not always openly honest with one another, and the school climate they may have come from was hostile and not inclusive or supportive. Be a different type of team that is inclusive and supportive. It's the only way the team will be impactful.

Now that the drivers have been addressed, we are ready to focus on Section III, which is the process for doing this work.

GUIDING QUESTIONS

- What does social sensitivity look like among your team? How is it respected?

- Why have school leaders been left out of the collective efficacy research?

- What are the four experiences that Albert Bandura's research shows have the most profound impact on fostering confidence among individuals and the whole instructional leadership team?

- What are some methods that teams can use to help individuals feel more comfortable contributing to their collectives?

What two questions do you wish I had asked?

1.

2.

What three new areas of learning did you experience while reading this chapter?

1.

2.

3.

SECTION III

DELIBERATE PRACTICE AND PROCESS

WHAT COMPONENTS DEFINE AN INSTRUCTIONAL CORE?

10

Everything should be anchored in the instructional core of schooling.

Richard Elmore (2006, p. 517)

THEORY OF ACTION

If . . . instructional leadership teams understand the three main components of the instructional core, then . . . they will be more likely to engage in initiatives that focus on learning.

GUIDING QUESTIONS

- In what ways did your leadership professional learning and development help prepare you for your present role?

- Richard Elmore believes that leadership professional learning and development is a catastrophe. Do you agree? Why or why not?

- How does your instructional leadership team focus on the knowledge and skills of teachers in ways that are nonjudgmental?

- In what ways are students encouraged in their own learning? How do you believe that is going?

- How do teachers in your school partner with students in delivering challenging content? What does that look like?

- How can assistant principals, instructional coaches, and teacher leaders impact the three main components of the instructional core?

As a former teacher and principal, I used many KWL charts with students. It was a great way to activate prior knowledge and gain an understanding of what they wanted to learn and not merely what I wanted to teach them. As we know, *K* stands for what we already *know* about the topic. *W* can either stand for what we *want* to learn or what we *wonder* about the topic. Lastly, *L* comes at the end of the learning and stands for what I have *learned*.

KWL charts engage us in a conceptual understanding of learning, so as we begin this section on practice and this particular chapter on the instructional core of a school, I want your team to engage in a conceptual activity referred to as CLICK (Activity 10.1). Take a few moments with your team to focus on the essential questions: What does student engagement look like? How should instructional leadership teams (ILTs) go about focusing on student engagement?

Activity 10.1
CLICK Exercise

CLICK is a process similar to a KWL chart (Stern, n. d.) It helps us build understanding around a concept or idea. Below, you will see that I wrote the essential question or concept. Please take some time to engage in the activity to activate your prior knowledge of instructional leadership.

Essential Question: What does student engagement look like? How should instructional leadership teams go about focusing on student engagement?				
C What **concepts** are central to this question?	**L** **List** everything you know about the concept.	**I** What **inquiries** do you have about the concept?	**C** What **evidence** from the contexts will help you answer the conceptual question?	**K** What do you already **know** about the relationship between these concepts?

BREAKING UP THE CARTEL OF SCHOOL LEADERSHIP

In a scathing article, Elmore (2006) wrote,

> It is no longer necessary to belabor the catastrophe that is the education, certification, and licensure of school leaders in the U.S. The cartel—the interlocking and self-perpetuating system of state agencies, cash-for-credit university programs, and hopelessly inadequate local hiring practices—has been exposed once again in all its gory detail, this time from within. (p. 517)

Elmore was referring to Arthur Levine's (2005) report titled *Educating School Leaders*. Elmore goes on to offer four principles to help break this "cartel" and improve school leadership. The first two principles are these:

> Principle 1. Everything should be anchored in the instructional core of schooling. Traditionally, the status of educational administrators has been defined by their distance from instructional practice.

> Principle 2. Systemic problems require systemic solutions. Districts typically have nothing resembling a human resource management strategy that would allow them to dictate requirements for prospective school leaders. (Elmore, 2006, p. 517)

The purpose of schooling is to have school leaders who have the credibility to practice instructional leadership. The time of sticking only to management practices should be over and done with these days. Our school issues are complicated, and we need leadership that will help improve them, not continue the status quo of accepting those issues.

> Principle 3. Professions have practices. Educational leadership is a profession without a practice (Elmore, 2006, p. 518).

What Elmore is referring to here is that there is no defined approach to school leadership in buildings and the profession needs to contribute to the development of impactful leadership. Gaining a license in school leadership is often about jumping through hoops, paying the bill for credit hours, and checking off the boxes that professors deem important; it's often not about developing a holistic approach to providing deep, impactful leadership.

It's not atypical for a school leader to win the building leader job after looking the best in an interview where they say the right things to the right people, get handed the keys, and then are left to their own devices. It's also not atypical for instructional coaches and teacher leaders to be chosen for their positions but not given many opportunities to engage in professional learning that focuses on how to do it effectively. In schools, leadership is often a guessing game when it comes to where exactly to start leading and how to best engage in the practice of leadership. I hope by writing this, I am not biting the hand that feeds me when it comes to those of you who are reading this book. However, for those of us who completed a degree in school leadership, we most likely had an experience that isn't too far off from what Elmore refers to in his article.

Elmore (2006, p. 518) continues, "Bottom line: If educators want to exercise political influence in the reconstitution of leadership, they will have to begin to act more like professionals. If they don't, plenty of people will gladly tell them what they should be doing." Elmore's last principle is as hard hitting as the first three:

> Principle 4. Powerful practices require strategies; a list is not a strategy. Educational administration programs are typically characterized by what might charitably be called "list logic": here is a list of courses, take some or all of them, do an internship, and, presto, you're qualified to be an administrator. (p. 518)

This process is about developing individual mindsets of leaders and developing the mindset of a team so that those individuals and teams can strengthen their instructional cores.

Elmore even goes on to say that the very popular Interstate School Leaders Licensure Consortium (ISLLC) is merely a list. It is partly due to Elmore's critique that I write this book.

Your ILT can have a positive impact on your school building. Elmore writes that everything about school leadership should be anchored in the instructional core, and I believe an ILT can provide the focus to make that happen. In schools, there is often a focus on adult issues, such as prep time (which is important), union relationships (which are important), and how teachers get along with families (which is important), but there needs to be a greater focus on learning.

This process is about developing individual mindsets of leaders and developing the mindset of a team so that those individuals and teams can strengthen their instructional cores.

REFLECT

How Prepared Are You to Be a School Leader?

Elmore offers a pretty scathing critique of school leadership preparation. Take a moment to reflect on the following questions, which will ultimately guide our ILTs thinking later on.

1. What else could your school leadership program have done to prepare you for the position?

2. If you are a teacher leader or instructional coach, what do you need to be better prepared as a leader?

3. Does your school district foster growth in its school leaders?

4. How do you foster growth in the members of your ILT? If this is a new team for you, what would you do first to help them grow as leaders?

WHAT CONSTITUTES AN INSTRUCTIONAL CORE?

Dufour (2002) wrote,

> This shift from a focus on teaching to a focus on learning is more than semantics. When learning becomes the preoccupation of the school, when all the school's educators examine the efforts and initiatives of the school through the lens of their impact on learning, the structure and culture of the school begin to change in substantive ways. (p. 13)

This shift that Dufour wrote about is what Elmore considers an instructional core.

A school community's instructional core includes three components that work interdependently. Those three components are (1) the teachers' knowledge and skills, (2) how students engage in their own learning, and (3) content that is academically challenging (Elmore, 2009).

All of these components are more than worthy of the attention of an ILT; they should be the three areas of focus for the ILT. Whether we think about content such as numeracy or literacy or even societal issues such as antiracist education, those will fit into each one of the components. In the following pages, I have taken time to separate each one and support them through deeper research and suggestions of actions to engage in as your team heads toward Section III of this book, which is completely focused on developing your plan.

TEACHERS' KNOWLEDGE AND SKILLS

It begins with teachers' knowledge and skills. This focus has been at the center of pre-service teaching programs for decades. It's the reason why prospective teachers have had to engage in methods courses and student teaching. As we know, just as with school building leadership practices, the knowledge and skills of teachers deepen as they gain experience in their profession. Your ILT can play an important role in this process.

But not every school building leader knows about these skills and knowledge. That is not a judgment as much as it is a starting point for a conversation. Even Dufour (2002, p. 13) wrote, "Eventually, after years as a principal, I realized that even though my efforts had been well intentioned—and even though I had devoted countless hours each school year to those efforts—I had been focusing on the wrong questions." Members of the ILT can share their knowledge to help alleviate this issue.

When it comes to the teachers' knowledge and skills, it's common to believe that subject-matter knowledge is the most important aspect. However, research suggests that there is another way to begin looking at the knowledge and skills of teachers. Hattie (2012) writes,

> In Visible Learning, it was shown that teachers' subject-matter knowledge had little effect on the quality of student outcomes! The distinction, however, is less the "amount" of knowledge and less the "pedagogical content knowledge," but more about how teachers see the surface and the deeper understandings of the subjects that they teach, as well as their beliefs about how to teach and understand when students are learning and have learned the subject. (p. 28)

Hattie (2012) goes on to offer five high levels of knowledge and understandings of what he refers to as "expert teachers." Those five dimensions include the following:

1. Expert teachers can identify the important ways in which they can represent the subject they teach.

2. Expert teachers are proficient at creating an optimal classroom climate for learning.

3. Expert teachers monitor learning and provide feedback.

4. Expert teachers believe that all students can reach the success criteria.

5. Expert teachers influence surface and deep student outcomes. (pp. 28–32)

When teachers can develop these five dimensions, it contributes to their level of credibility among students. Hattie and Yates (2014) write,

> It has been established that students will rate their best teachers highly on traits such as competency, credibility, and fairness. Such traits appear more strongly linked to student motivation than to actual learning. Notably, students value the interaction and feedback received from teachers they recognize as clever and knowledgeable adults. (p. 13)

This notion of students feeling highly motivated by such teachers is called *teacher credibility*. Fisher et al. (2016, p. 11) write, "Students know which teachers can make a difference in their lives. Teacher credibility is a constellation of characteristics, including trust, competence, dynamism, and immediacy. Students evaluate each of these factors to determine if their teacher is credible."

The process of understanding teachers' knowledge and skills, as well as the importance of teacher credibility among students, can be easily examined when ILTs engage in learning walks, flipped faculty meetings, and learning-centered department and grade-level meetings. Additionally, understanding teachers' knowledge and skills is supported through formal and informal teacher observations that foster dialogue among the school leader and teachers involved.

To help your ILT with these practices and processes, I offer Activity 10.2.

Activity 10.2 Gathering Data to Align Practices With the Instructional Core

Use formal meetings (i.e., department meetings, grade-level meetings, faculty meetings) to take part in nonjudgmental discussions about the ways that teachers engage students through social-emotional and academic learning. Ask the following questions:

- What actions do teachers take to engage their students through social-emotional and academic methods?

- What instructional strategies do teachers in our grade-level or department use to meet the needs of all learners in their classrooms?

 **NOTES**

Teachers' knowledge and skills intersect with student engagement. The more expertise a teacher has, the greater chance that a variety of student engagement methods are being used in their classroom. Gathering that evidence will better prepare your ILT to focus on the direction of their theory of action.

STUDENT ENGAGEMENT

According to Nuthall (2007), there are three worlds that exist within a classroom:

Public world: "Which the teacher sees and manages."

Semi-private world: "Ongoing peer relationships." This is the world in which students maintain their social roles and status.

Private world: The child's own private mind. "This is where children's knowledge and beliefs change and grow." (p. 84)

It's really no wonder that student engagement can be such a tricky topic when all three of these worlds are happening simultaneously in a classroom.

For too long, school leaders and teachers focused on time on task, and as you can see from the work of Nuthall (2007), students may seem to be on task, but the impact of the learning will really depend on what world they are in. Just because a student looks like they are on task does not mean they are actually involved in surface, deep, or transfer learning, and just because a student is in the primary grades doesn't mean they cannot engage in deep learning. Equally as important is that just because students are in secondary school doesn't mean they do not need some level of surface learning.

What makes student engagement even more complex is that time on task can often be code from the adults that really means, "The students are quiet and I, as the teacher, have good classroom management." For full disclosure, when I was a young teacher, I learned more about classroom management techniques geared in compliance than I did about academically engaging techniques to use in the classroom. The reason was that a teacher who sends students to the principal's office is seen as a teacher who cannot control their classroom, so therefore control in the classroom outweighed any other technique. This is a good place to pause and engage in a student council reflection.

STUDENT COUNCIL REFLECTION

How can students engage in developing a deeper understanding of the types of learning environments that exists in your school community?

What types of discussions has your ILT had with students to gain an understanding of the student perspective of how students engage in their own learning?

Have there been specific moments dedicated to asking students what the learning environment in the school actually looks like?

Additionally, what makes student engagement so interesting is that it is often looked at as what the teacher provides to the student to engage those students in learning experiences. As Nuthall (2007, p. 156) found, "A large proportion of a student's significant learning experience is self-selected or self-generated rather than stemming directly from the teacher." So, the question becomes, how can we use the research behind what engagement looks like to better understand how to set up learning experiences within our classrooms? Is there something teachers need to do differently during synchronous and asynchronous learning that will help in this self-selection of learning?

Fredricks et al. (2004, p. 60) found that research literature defines *student engagement* in three ways. The first level of engagement is "behavioral engagement, [which] draws on the idea of participation." Fredricks et al. go on to say that behavioral engagement "includes involvement in academic and social or extracurricular activities and is considered crucial for achieving positive academic outcomes and pre-venting dropping out." The second type of engagement is "emotional engagement, [which] encompasses positive and negative reactions to teachers, classmates, academics, and school and is presumed to create ties to an institution and influence willingness to do the work." Lastly, there is "cognitive engagement, [which] draws on the idea of invest-ment; it incorporates thoughtfulness and willingness to exert the effort necessary to comprehend complex ideas and master difficult skills."

Although there are nuances of each type of engagement (such as the fact that behavioral engagement may inspire compliant learning over authentic learning), it does give us the ability to start to craft our understanding of student engagement. Fredricks et al. (2004, p. 85) leave us with some inquiry-based questions that our ILTs should ponder:

1. Which types of engagement are more likely to be displayed during the early grades?

2. How do the three types of engagement evolve and change over time?

3. Are any aspects of context more important among some age groups than others?

The question now becomes, what does this look like in your school? If members of your team have spent time engaging in walk-throughs, which are less than 10 minutes and do not involve giving feedback to teachers, or learning walks, which are more than 10 minutes and involve providing feedback, this should be a simple question to answer. If members of teams have not engaged in walk-throughs or learning walks, it's time to consider beginning the process of engaging in them.

In Activity 10.3, I am asking that members of your team engage in walk-throughs. If your team has been doing walk-throughs, then go ahead and jump into the activity. If your team has not been doing walk-throughs, then it might be best to involve staff in the discussion about why you are now doing them now.

 # Activity 10.3 Observe Student Engagement

With a partner or team, visit three different classrooms within your school. Each member of your team can walk into three different classrooms or the same three classrooms. Spend 10 minutes in each classroom. Come back together and discuss the following:

1. Out of the three types of engagement researched by Fredricks et al. (2004), which types of engagement are more likely to be displayed in your school?

2. How have you seen the three types of engagement evolve and change over time?

3. Are any aspects of context more important among some of your grade levels or student population than others?

Disclaimer: This activity is a lot easier to accomplish if your team has been involved in learning walks. If your team has not been involved in learning walks, begin thinking about how you can engage in learning walks with teachers in your school.

NOTES

When taking cognitive engagement into account, Doyle (1983, p. 160) found that schooling went from placing emphasis on "punctuality, patience, production schedules, and obedience, [providing] training in a work ethic uniquely suited to the requirements of an industrialized society" to focusing on content and curriculum as a collection of tasks in which students show depth of understanding. That curriculum and content typically focus attention on three different aspects of students' work:

> (a) the products students are to formulate, such as an original essay or answers to a set of test questions; (b) the operations that are to be used to generate the product, such as memorizing a list of words; and (c) the "givens" or resources available to students while they are generating a product, such as a model of a finished essay. (p. 160)

Doyle (1983, p. 161) goes on to say, "Academic tasks, in other words, are defined by the answers students are required to produce and the routes that can be used to obtain these answers." The issue here is that student engagement is too often focused on what the adult in the room wants and not necessarily on what the student deems to be important. This is important to think about because Nuthall's work shows that a large percentage of impactful student learning is self-selected. Nuthall (2007, p. 156) found that "the students learned, on average, about half the concepts they learned because they were able to self-select or self-generate the activities." This may mean that the core content doesn't change but how students engage in learning about that content does.

ACADEMICALLY CHALLENGING CONTENT

For students to be able to move about their learning independently, we need to understand not only the need for challenging content but also the reasoning behind its importance. Academically challenging content, which an ILT can develop together, is interrelated with cognitive load. *Cognitive load* is related to the amount of information that our working memory can hold at one particular time. Researchers suggest that since our working memory has a limited capacity, our instructional strategies should avoid overloading that working memory with additional strategies or activities that don't directly contribute to learning.

Hattie and Yates (2014) write,

> The CLT [Cognitive Load Theory] research has been of special interest to educators for two principal reasons: (a) it directly addresses the problem of why learning is so inherently difficult for human beings, and (b) it specifies how teachers and instructional designers can make it relatively easier for students to learn and store new information. (p. 146)

Given the research behind cognitive load and the two principal reasons laid out by Hattie and Yates (2014), it explains why strategies such as teacher clarity are so impactful when discussing academically challenging content. One of the steps in teacher clarity is that of task orientation, which consists of talking only about those things related to the topic (Bush et al., 1977).

I realize that is a difficult and challenging concept to approach in a mere few paragraphs of a book, but if ILTs are to strengthen their instructional core by offering more academically challenging content to students, which will ultimately support the student's independent learning and growth, then we have to provide an overview here.

Learning is not always easy—nor should it be. Students and adults alike should always experience learning as a balance between easy and hard, but giving into learning because it's too hard is not a concept we should easily accept. There should be many open discussions among an ILT about the difference between content that is impossible and content that is very difficult and may take time. ILTs can ultimately use this as part of their leadership team discussions and core focus.

What is needed more in schools is knowledge building in the cognitive load process, which happens when instructional practices help learners "mindfully combine simple ideas into more complex schemata" (Hattie & Yates, 2014, p. 147). Czarnec and Hill (2018) write,

> One particular aspect of learning that instructors should consider is how students use prior knowledge to comprehend and learn from text. Schema Theory emphasizes the mental connections learners make between pieces of information and can be a very powerful component of the learning process.

This process can create the right conditions for students to become curious in their own learning. In an interview with Harvard Graduate School professor Elizabeth Bonawitz, *Mindshift*'s Nimah Gobir (2020) writes,

> Curiosity is not a trait that is "fostered" in children. It isn't like a set of skills that can be taught because it exists in each and every one of us. Curiosity needs the right conditions and encouragement, so instead of focusing on how to create more curious young people, educators can concentrate on developing opportunities for students to be curious.

To build schema and knowledge, teachers and leaders need to understand that words are not enough. Words alone don't create the conditions necessary for students to be curious. There need to be multiple modalities in order to build knowledge and offer challenging curriculum. Hattie and Yates (2014) go on to offer principles that are needed to advance more challenging content that will increase cognitive load:

- **Worked examples.** As novices, students need to see how knowledge applies to specific cases.

- **Multimedia.** We learn better when words accompany pictures rather than words alone.

- **Contiguity.** Words should be placed as close to the relevant defining image as possible.

- **Coherence**. We learn better when extraneous information is removed.

- **Modality**. We learn better when we listen to words in combination with images. (p. 150)

Additionally, in order to offer challenging curriculum, we need to understand the importance of cognitive load, building schema, and how to present that challenging curriculum. ILTs are key to this process, but the ILT doesn't always have the credibility to pursue these instructional core topics. Each member of the team needs to practice instructional leadership in order to engage in conversations and actionable steps focusing on their school's instructional core.

IN THE END

Elmore isn't the first to emphasize a focus on an instructional core. In his instructional leadership research, Edmonds (1979) concentrated on commonalities among what constitutes a focus on learning. Those commonalities are

- fostering teachers' professional learning and growth,

- facilitating work around teachers and building goals,

- fostering school climate, and

- implementing curriculum in classrooms and grade levels that will ultimately have an impact on student engagement (Robinson et al., 2008, pp. 638–639; Salo et al., 2015, p. 491; Southworth, 2002, pp. 76–86).

This chapter focuses on the meaning of the instructional core and the three components to develop that core within schools. Those components are (1) teachers' knowledge and skills, (2) student engagement, and (3) academically engaging content. It is not easy work, but the conversations needed to engage in that work include issues of self-efficacy, collective leader efficacy, and our own preparation for this work.

ILTs can have a big impact on these three components of an instructional core by focusing on topics such as the authentic learning experiences that students and teachers can engage in with one another. ILTs can only do that when members of the team step up to take the lead and engage in these conversations with their students, families, and colleagues. In order to do this work, ILTs need to understand their specific focus and how conversations around student engagement fit into the context of their school. The best way to foster these discussions and create an actionable plan is by engaging in a cycle of inquiry, which is the focus of the next chapter.

At the beginning of the book, I warned teams that this book involved doing the actual work, which is why there have been so many activities meant to deepen their focus as a team. The inquiry cycle in the next chapter will involve a great deal of work on the part of the team, so please be prepared. This is where inquiry meets curiosity, and we need more of that in school.

GUIDING QUESTIONS

- In what ways did your leadership professional learning and development help prepare you for your present role?

- Richard Elmore believes that leadership professional learning and development is a catastrophe. Do you agree? Why or why not?

- How does your instructional leadership team focus on the knowledge and skills of teachers in ways that are nonjudgmental?

- In what ways are students encouraged in their own learning? How do you believe that is going?

- How do teachers in your school partner with students in delivering challenging content? What does that look like?

- How can assistant principals, instructional coaches, and teacher leaders impact the three main components of the instructional core?

What two questions do you wish I had asked?

1.

2.

What three new areas of learning did you experience while reading this chapter?

1.

2.

3.

NOTES

THE INSTRUCTIONAL LEADERSHIP TEAM'S CYCLE OF INQUIRY

11

We are all participants in inquiry, not spectators:
We change a problematic situation and are changed
in turn through our actions.

Leo Casey and Bertram Bruce (2011)

THEORY OF ACTION

If instructional leadership teams engage in a cycle of inquiry together . . . then collective leader efficacy will be fostered and a deeper impact on learning is more likely to take place.

GUIDING QUESTIONS

- How does your instructional leadership team practice the two types of organizational learning?

- How will a cycle of inquiry help your team in the improvement process?

- Using the four questions to guide the cycle of inquiry, what specific inquiry questions did you develop as a team?

- How do you hope those inquiry questions will impact your school community in a positive way?

CYCLE OF INQUIRY

How do teachers, instructional coaches, assistant principals, and school building leaders within your organization best learn? Over the course of this book, my hope is that your team has engaged in learning about collective leader efficacy and the various drivers but also about your specific focus on learning. What are the needs of your school community? What are you curious about concerning learning? I often worry that adults spend so much time going into their classrooms and schools to teach that they forget that they are also there to learn.

Not only has this book focused on how your leadership team functions and learns together, but it has also focused on the importance of student learning and the journey from surface learning to deep learning and transfer-level learning.

We have now gotten to the point where your team begins their specific focus on learning and puts theory into action. At its core, this book is about how your individual organization learns together, and the last two chapters of this book will take that learning and put it into action.

Organizational learning is important, and it's not merely a topic for researchers or school leadership classes. Organizational learning research is about how schools, with all of the adults and students within them, choose to learn. Robinson (2001, p. 58) found that "there are two distinct strands of research on organisational learning. The descriptive strand, with its roots in social and cognitive psychology, seeks to understand the processes by which organisations learn and adapt." We have spent a great deal of time concentrating on that aspect of organizational leadership because social and cognitive theory are at the heart of self-efficacy, collective teacher efficacy, collective leader efficacy, and Bandura's (1997) work on each of those.

Additional to the descriptive strand is the normative strand of organizational learning. Robinson (2001, p. 58) found that "the normative strand, which is sometimes referred to as research on the 'learning organization,' is concerned more with how organisations can direct their learning in ways that bring them closer to an ideal." And that research on the normative strand of organizational learning is what brings us to this chapter on a cycle of inquiry.

In order for your instructional leadership team (ILT) to bond closer together, have a positive impact on the learning that takes place in your school, and develop collective leader efficacy, they will need to enter into cycles of inquiry. Cycles of inquiry are meant to assist teams in directing the learning of individuals and teams within their organizations. Keep in mind, this whole book has centered around collaboration and the voices of everyone on the team, so do not be scared of the fact that I just used the word *directing* in that last sentence.

Casey (2014) writes, "Questions are the root of inquiry; they initiate, sustain and invigorate each aspect of the process. Questions direct investigation, drive creativity, stimulate discussion, and are the bedrock of reflection" (p. 510). Casey goes on to write, "When we describe learning in terms of inquiry, we are clearly affirming that learning and questioning processes are somehow intertwined" (p. 510). The reality is that individuals on the team are inquisitive, or at least, they felt inquisitive at one time in their lives. Our ILTs need to find a place that brings that curiosity to the table and gain an understanding of what is working and what is not within their building.

Cycles of inquiry are inspired from the work of Dewey (1956), who purported that there are four primary interests of a learner (both child and adult). Those four interests are inquiry, communication, construction, and expression. Inquiry is inspired by questions we want to ask. Communication is a person's need to engage in social relationships, which we explored earlier with self-efficacy and its place in social cognitive theory. Construction is a person or team's need to build something, and reflection is understanding the meaning behind the experience they have had.

Casey and Bruce (2011, pp. 78-79) write, "We need to interpret the cycle as suggestive, neither the sole, nor the complete, characterisation of inquiry-based learning. Inquiry rarely proceeds in a simple, linear fashion." Additionally, I think it's important to mention here that this doesn't have to be a stiff process. We hear terms such as *inquiry* or *linear process* and our minds go to a place where everyone is serious and chooses their words carefully.

This process should be engaging, somewhat fun, and even messy at times. I think we can still have fun while we are engaging in deep learning about the instructional core of our school. As Donohoo (2013, p. 23) says, "Inquiry should be viewed primarily as a professional learning strategy as opposed to a research design."

When it comes to the inquiry process, Casey and Bruce (2011) go on to write,

> Each step can be embedded in any of the others, and so on. In fact, the very nature of inquiry is that these steps are mutually reinforcing and interrelated. Together, they comprise a cycle that can be used to inform and guide educational experiences for learners. (p. 79)

Given all of the research on the profound impact that a cycle of inquiry can have on individuals and groups, I have created a cycle of inquiry for your team. This cycle of inquiry has been used by instructional coaches and leadership coaches in my on-demand courses, and it has been used with groups at workshops that I coach. As you will see in Figure 11.1, the cycle of inquiry has six elements to it. Take some time with your team to look at the image. I will explain each aspect of the cycle of inquiry below.

Figure 11.1 Cycle of Inquiry Model

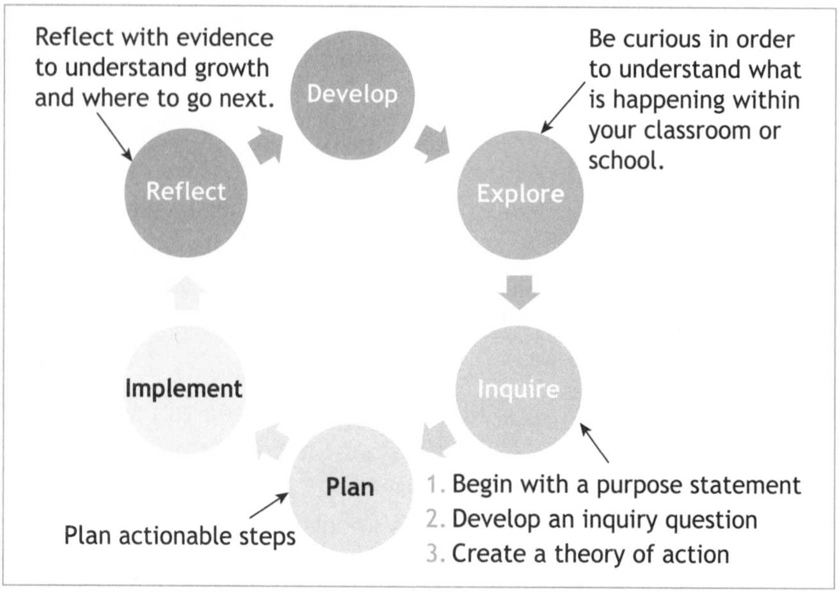

Reflect with evidence to understand growth and where to go next.

Develop

Be curious in order to understand what is happening within your classroom or school.

Reflect

Explore

Implement

Inquire

Plan

1. Begin with a purpose statement
2. Develop an inquiry question
3. Create a theory of action

Plan actionable steps

Source: DeWitt, 2021.

There are six steps in the cycle of inquiry:

Develop. It's important that your ILT develops an understanding of how the team will work together when it comes to a focus on learning. Pay close attention to a couple of these questions because you will see them again.

- How do we develop a shared understanding of student engagement?
- How do we develop a shared understanding of how students and teachers are engaged in authentic learning experiences?
- How do we develop an understanding of how the ILT supports students and teachers in that pursuit?

Explore. ILTs need to understand how they are presently doing the work that they referred to in the development stage. It's important that ILTs do not reinvent the wheel, especially if they are already engaged in actions that are impactful. Keep the following questions in mind:

- How do we support students and teachers in their pursuit of authentic learning experiences?
- How do we provide equitable resources to our students and teachers so they can engage in authentic learning experiences?
- How can we improve in the way we engage our students and teachers?

Inquire. Later in this chapter, we will break this down even more, but *inquire* means that we engage in three specific actions:

- Develop a purpose statement that is inspired by a problem within the classroom or school.
- Take the purpose statement and create an inquiry question.
- Take the purpose statement and inquiry question and develop a theory of action.

Plan. In Chapter 12, we will focus on this aspect of the cycle of inquiry. Planning involves using a program logic model from which the ILT will take their theory of action and start to gain an understanding of what resources they will need, develop some impactful activities that will help them achieve their goal, create a timetable to hold themselves accountable, and gather evidence to understand the impact.

Implement. This aspect is when members of the ILT take those activities discussed in the program logic model, look at the timetable that they agreed upon, and begin taking actionable steps by putting those activities into action.

Reflect. The ILT needs to take time to reflect on their actions, gather evidence, and understand their impact.

As you can see, the first step in the inquiry process is to develop an understanding by asking questions, and as with all inquiry models, students must be at the center of the discussion. As I asked earlier, wouldn't it be impactful to have a student council engage in a cycle of inquiry? I will highlight what that might look like in some examples below. Investigate, create, discuss, and reflect will be explained further in Chapter 12.

It's important to note that there are many inquiry models, and some are referred to as *spirals of inquiry*. The bottom line at the heart of any inquiry is how a team focuses on student learning and involves students in the process. A cycle of inquiry is not merely how adults come together and talk about how students should learn.

Therefore, I have developed four guiding questions that need to be a part of the inquiry process, and if your team feels comfortable with them, they could be used in the development stage of the inquiry cycle. I highly suggest starting with the first three questions and using the fourth question for the reflecting stage of the cycle of inquiry.

These questions will help ILTs investigate what is happening in their schools and help to create hands-on learning experiences that foster the growth of students, teachers, and leaders. These questions should inspire deep discussion, which is why we focused on the drivers to developing your team in Section II—so you feel comfortable challenging each other's thinking. Finally, this process will inspire the ILT to reflect on what worked, what did not work, and where to go next when it comes to student learning.

FOUR QUESTIONS TO GUIDE THE CYCLE OF INQUIRY

To develop the cycle of inquiry in which teams learn through a process, it is important that they engage in discussions around learning. Those discussions require questions in order to develop an understanding of the focus of the work, and that is where we are now. Through my work with leadership teams and facilitating workshops as well as doing research, I have developed four guiding questions to help lead your ILT. These four questions intersect with Elmore's (2009) three components to the instructional core, but they also intersect with research about deep learning and social-emotional learning as well.

Throughout the book, we have explored ways that student councils can be included in the discussion on student learning. The reality is that progressive schools can include their student council in this process, and the four guiding questions can be as easily answered by those students as they can be by adults. If a student council approach is not possible, then perhaps two students can be a part of the ILT discussion, which was a suggestion made when we discussed roles on a team.

QUESTIONS TO GUIDE THE CYCLE OF INQUIRY

1. How are students and teachers working together to create authentic learning experiences?

2. How are we supporting students and teachers in that process?

3. How do we engage families in the process?

4. What unbiased evidence do we collect to understand our impact?

Let's take a moment to explore each one of the guiding questions. Please keep in mind that the short descriptions below are from my perspective, so feel free to expand on these descriptions by adding your own specific contextual perspective.

1. **How are students and teachers working together to create authentic learning experiences?**

There has been plenty of focus on student engagement and student learning throughout this book. Now it is up to your team, with the help of student input (through student council or student members on the ILT), to develop a common language and a common under-standing about what you believe *authentic learning* means. I believe it means we want to engage in experiences with students that will encourage them to think for themselves. This, of course, intersects with Elmore's research about students engaging in their own learning but additionally takes into account a teacher's knowledge and skill. After all, teachers need the knowledge and skill to be able to do this work. However, not only do teachers need to understand how this is done—school building leaders do as well.

As your team engages in learning walks, this question is one that should be used to maintain your focus as you walk from one class to the next. It means taking into account student voice, surface- to deep-level learning, deficit thinking, the knowledge dimensions that have been explored in this book, and discussions about equity and anti-racism. This is an important time to help create those authentic experiences with students.

2. How are we supporting students and teachers in that process?

Throughout the book, we have focused on ways to elevate the voices of students and teachers, and we covered professional learning and development as a necessary driver to building collective leader efficacy among the ILT. You were even provided with activities that you can use with your ILT or with teachers in faculty meetings. Additionally, we included Robinson's work on promoting and participating in teacher learning and development.

During these stressful times, we know that well-being is important, so social-emotional support is important, too. Given all that we have concentrated on, what is your ILT doing to support teachers from an academic and social-emotional standpoint? Perhaps this is where your ILT begins to focus on de-implementation rather than implementation.

What we know is that from an academic standpoint, we can always go deeper when it comes to student learning. De-implementation can allow the ILT to work with teachers in the school on high-impact teaching strategies that will encourage and foster deeper learning. What this means, and the reason why I mention de-implementation is that ILT's can engage in dialogue and professional learning and development that will allow teachers to suspend the use of strategies that are just not that engaging.

Lastly, de-implementation will help the social-emotional issues teachers and students face because it fosters a "less is more" philosophy which could alleviate the stress everyone feels.

3. How do we engage families in the process?

School communication usually comes in three different forms. Those forms are informational, dialogical, and learning (DeWitt, 2019b). Informational communication includes the use of newsletters or posts on social media to provide important dates and times. Open house at the beginning of the year, when teachers meet parents for the first time, tends to be informational as opposed to dialogical.

Dialogical communication is when teachers and parents have time to talk with one another, such as during parent-teacher conferences, when the student's report card is the center of attention. As a school principal, I began sending report cards home a week ahead of time so parents had time to look at them instead of receiving them at the meeting (when they wouldn't have time to prepare any questions). At first, some teachers worried that parents wouldn't come to their designated time if they already had received the report card, but holding a report card hostage in order to coerce parents to come in is not the way to build a relationship. We even provided parents with sample questions they could ask their child's teacher.

Learning typically encompasses special events such as math nights, science fairs, chorus and band concerts, art exhibitions, or maker space nights. Too often, communication to families is overloaded with one-sided informational messages and does not come in forms that encourage dialogue and learning.

4. What unbiased evidence do we collect to understand our impact?

What evidence does your ILT collect that would offer an unbiased opinion of the impact your team is having on the school community? Confirmation bias happens when we look for evidence that will directly support our opinions. It is natural for all of us to specifically look for evidence that will support our opinions.

For example, I engage in a lot of learning walks with school leaders and we are constantly at risk of having a learning walk bias. What does this look like? As a former first-grade teacher, I walk into first-grade classrooms expecting to see a classroom set up similar to how mine was when I was a teacher. It does not mean I believe I was the greatest teacher in the world, but I spent so many years in the role that it is very difficult for me to let go of the image I have in my head of a first-grade classroom. I have had to learn to suspend my bias when I walk into classrooms to make sure I am getting a fresh perspective and not merely looking for issues that will confirm my bias.

Triangulating data is the best way to move forward. Anderson et al. (1991, p. 53) write that triangulation brings together several sources of information. Heal and Forbes (2013) write,

> Triangulation in research is the use of more than one approach to researching a question. The objective is to increase confidence in the findings through the confirmation of a proposition using two or more independent measures. The combination of findings from two or more rigorous approaches provides a more comprehensive picture of the results than either approach could do alone. (p. 98)

For our purposes, triangulation will allow your ILT to understand impact. The ILT can look at the evidence collected from learning walks and formative assessment data collected from teachers and student data such as surveys, exit tickets, authentic assessments, student voice groups, and portfolios. In Appendix 4, your team will find a sample of a learning walk document.

WHAT IS OUR PURPOSE?

Taking our cue from the guiding questions I developed, let's connect that concept with the next step in this inquiry process. We will ultimately use all four questions in the inquiry process but it's the first three specifically that you will see in the section below as we develop purpose statements.

Donohoo (2013, p. 22) says, "Outlining a clear and compelling purpose for the collaborative effort will further inspire and motivate the team." It is important to choose wisely when it comes to the purpose statement because Donohoo writes that because it "sets the direction for data collection and reporting, it is important to use language that is exploratory in nature" (p. 23). That discussion around data is where the fourth question in the list of guiding questions enters into the process.

It's always good to have some practice before we enter into the deeper work. Your team needs time to wrap their heads around the process, especially if they are new to it. The following is an activity to help get your team started in the inquiry process. It begins with developing a purpose statement, and in the examples below, I will offer one suggestion for each of the guided questions introduced above and then provide you with the opportunity to create one as a team.

In the appendices of the book, your team will find templates you can use to engage in this process as you will actually use it in your school. This practice section is just that—it is practice. However, when you actually begin to develop purpose statements, questions, and theories of actions, you will need to set aside several of your ILT meetings in order to do that.

When it comes to creating purpose statements, Donohoo (2013, p. 24) suggests a kind of a formula for writing a purpose statement: You should ask whether the purpose is for participants to explore, discover, describe, or understand a specific issue. The examples provided below can also be used by your student council if you choose to bring them into the process.

After you work through each practice activity (Activity 11.1–11.3), please keep in mind the specific needs of your school.

 # Activity 11.1 Purpose Statement

Authentic Learning Experiences

Practice #1. Purpose Statement

Guiding Question #1: How are students and teachers working together to create authentic learning experiences?

Sample Problem Framed: In walk-throughs and formal observations, we notice that many students are engaged in surface-level work and we want students to experience deeper learning.

Purpose Statement: The purpose of this inquiry is to discover how often our students and teachers engage in deep and transfer-level learning.

Your Team's Turn:

Guiding Question #1: How are students and teachers working together to create authentic learning experiences?

Problem Framed:

Purpose Statement:

Activity 11.2 Purpose Statement

Supporting Students and Teachers

Practice #2. Purpose Statement

Guiding Question #2: How do we support students and teachers in this process?

Sample Problem Framed: We offer opportunities for teachers to attend professional development but are not sure that the professional development they attend has an impact on teacher and student practices in the classroom.

Purpose Statement. The purpose of this inquiry is to explore more impactful professional learning and development practices that will have a deeper impact on teaching and learning in classrooms.

Your Team's Turn:

Guiding Question #2: How do we support students and teachers in this process?

Problem Framed:

Purpose Statement:

Activity 11.3 Purpose Statement

Engaging Families

Practice #3. Purpose Statement

Guiding Question #3: How do we engage families in this process?

Sample Problem Framed: When looking at our communication as a school, we spend more time talking *at* families than we do talking *with* them.

Purpose Statement: The purpose of this inquiry is to develop better strategies to engage families in dialogue around student learning.

Your Team's Turn:

Guiding Question #3: How do we engage families in this process?

Problem Framed:

Purpose Statement:

As you can imagine, it would be enlightening to see what purpose statements a student council develops around these three specific questions. Would their purpose statements be different from the ones an ILT develops?

Now that we have established the purpose statements for your ILT's inquiry cycles, it is time to move on to developing inquiry questions from those purpose statements. As mentioned above, the fourth question (focusing on collecting unbiased evidence) is not included in the purpose statement practice section. That question will appear in the next section, in which your team will develop their own inquiry questions.

In the practice sections below (Activities 11.4–11.6), I will provide sample inquiry questions around the three questions that ILTs must ask. As stated before, the evidence question, which is number four on the list, will appear in each activity. Once again, Donohoo's (2013) work is highly impactful here:

> Use neutral exploratory language.

> Begin with the words *how* or *what*.

> Specify one adult action/change in practice.

> Specify one student learning outcome (p. 25).

Activity 11.4 Developing an Inquiry Question

Authentic Learning Experiences

Practice #1. Developing an Inquiry Question

Guiding Question #1: Authentic learning experiences

Possible Inquiry Question: How do teachers, leaders, and students define deep and transfer-level learning experiences?

Evidence: What evidence can we collect to help us gain that understanding?

Your Team's Turn:

Guiding Question #1: Authentic learning experiences

Possible Inquiry Questions:

Evidence:

Activity 11.5 Developing an Inquiry Question

Supporting Students and Teachers

Practice #2. Developing an Inquiry Question

Guiding Question #2: How do we support students and teachers in the process?

Possible Inquiry Question: What professional learning and development experiences can we create as a school community to support students and teachers in their development around authentic learning experiences?

Evidence:

Your Team's Turn:

Guiding Question #2: How do we support students and teachers in the process?

Possible Inquiry Questions:

Evidence:

Activity 11.6 Developing an Inquiry Question

Engaging Families

Practice #3. Developing an Inquiry Question

Guiding Question#3: How do we engage families in this process?

Possible Inquiry Question: In what ways do we engage families in discussions that focus on what and how their children learn?

Evidence:

Your Team's Turn:

Guiding Question #3: How do we engage families in this process?

Possible Inquiry Questions:

Evidence:

After you read the final section in this chapter, go to Appendices 7 and 8 to find the blank templates that will help you begin the process of developing purpose statements and inquiry questions. In the practice session, I have provided a space to jot down possible evidence you could collect to gain an understanding of each inquiry question.

IN THE END

Chapter 11 offered opportunities for heavy lifting on the part of your ILT. I understand that it was a lot to think about, but improvement is not easy. It's the reason why Bandura (1997) highlights mastery experiences as the most profound way to develop self-efficacy and collective efficacy. It takes time and plenty of dialogue. The first aspect of the inquiry process (asking questions) is definitely something that takes time. Your team may need to set aside a few instructional leadership sessions to engage in the work. In the next chapter, I will offer you a sample timetable to engage in this work.

It is now time to take the work your team did around purpose statements and inquiry questions and develop a theory of action. As your team develops a theory of action, we will bring in the next parts of a cycle of inquiry, which are to investigate, create, discuss, and reflect on the ways that the theory of action is being implemented.

Additionally, in Chapter 12, you will be introduced to a specific program logic model that will help lead you to the necessary actions to carry out the improvement process as well as give you specific ideas about what actions to use.

GUIDING QUESTIONS

- How does your instructional leadership team practice the two types of organizational learning?
- How will a cycle of inquiry help your team in the improvement process?
- Using the four questions to guide the cycle of inquiry, what specific inquiry questions did you develop as a team?
- How do you hope those inquiry questions will impact your school community in a positive way?

What two questions do you wish I had asked?

1.

2.

What three new areas of learning did you experience while reading this chapter?

1.

2.

3.

NOTES

FOCUS FOR IMPROVEMENT

To lead improvement is to exercise influence in ways that leave the team, organization, or system in a better state than before.

Viviane Robinson (2018, p. 2)

THEORY OF ACTION

If . . . a team uses a theory of action to approach implementation, then . . . they will be more likely to develop a more proactive approach to improvement.

GUIDING QUESTIONS

- Why is it important for an instructional leadership team to process what improvement initiatives look like?

- When research says *strategic resourcing*, what does that mean?

- Why are some schools activity rich and impact poor?

- Why does an instructional leadership team need to develop a timetable?

- Why is it that some schools are awash with data but do very little with that data?

- Where does evidence fit into your instructional leadership team's improvement process?

PUTTING IT ALL TOGETHER

In Chapter 11, I introduced you to the cycle of inquiry. As I mentioned before, cycles of inquiry are all about being curious—curious about what we have been doing and whether those actions have had an impact on learning and curious about new strategies we can explore.

That cycle of inquiry that I introduced you to in Chapter 11 is once again pictured below (Figure 12.1).

Figure 12.1 Cycle of Inquiry Model

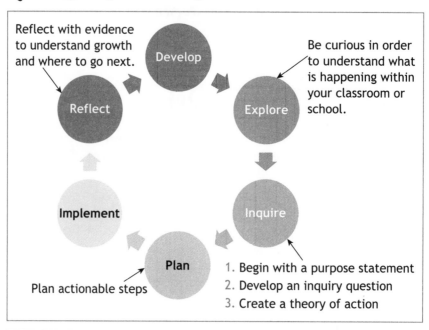

Source: DeWitt, 2021.

In Section I, we discussed developing collective leader efficacy through our instructional leadership teams (ILTs). It was in that chapter that I asked you to consider how students can be involved in the process of improvement within your school community. I realize that a student council is not an example of collective leader efficacy because those councils do not consist of school-based professionals only, but they may be an important part of the improvement process because we know that students can provide us with a lot of important insight.

Section II was all about the drivers needed to develop as an ILT and build collective leader efficacy together. As a sort of sidebar,

I provided ways for student councils to use the information to develop stronger teams. The drivers that I proposed in this book are meant to help teams function together, understand one another, and learn with each other. Perhaps your team already did a few of those very well and needed to go more in-depth with a few others or perhaps your team needed to engage with each and every one of the drivers. Either way, my hope is that they helped you come together as a more productive, inclusive, and curious team.

Now it is time to continue with the moderately heavy lifting that I mentioned in Chapter 11. We will take the cycle of inquiry and the development of purpose statements and inquiry questions and bring them into this chapter so that your team can create a theory of action.

DEVELOPING A THEORY OF ACTION

Donohoo (2013, p. 27) writes, "Theories of action come in two types: espoused theories (stated as beliefs and values) and theories-in-use (actual behavior)." If we look at our beliefs and our actions, we will all find that there are times when our actions do not line up with our beliefs. For example, in my instructional leadership work, I have had the honor of working with thousands of school leaders, and a vast majority of them believe they are instructional leaders. Unfortunately, when we begin to dive into the research behind instructional leadership and what it looks like in action, I find that those same leaders lack the consistency needed to practice it, so their actions do not match up to their beliefs. I have surveyed hundreds and hundreds of principals and a vast majority of them answered that they are very confident they are instructional leaders, but when surveying teachers, I have found that a majority of those teachers were only somewhat confident or not confident at all that their school-based leaders were instructional leaders.

In the following activities (Activity 12.1-12.3), we will develop a theory of action, which will help marry our beliefs and our actions so there is less of a gap between the two.

As in previous sections, I will provide some examples based on our previous problems and then will provide a space for your ILT to practice developing their own theory of action. In Appendix 9, your team also will find a sample and a blank template to use when you are prepared to engage in the improvements you would like to establish in your school community.

Activity 12.1 Theory of Action

Authentic Learning Experiences

Example:

Theory of Action

If . . . (Action),

Then . . . (Outcome).

Guiding Question #1: How are students and teachers working together to create authentic learning experiences?

Sample Problem Framed: In walk-throughs and formal observations, we notice that many students are engaged in surface-level work; we want students to experience deeper learning.

Purpose Statement: The purpose of this inquiry is to discover how often our students and teachers engage in deep and transfer-level learning.

Possible Inquiry Question(s):

1. How do teachers, leaders, and students define deep and transfer-level learning experiences?

Evidence. What evidence can we collect to help us gain that understanding?

If we can develop a common language and common understanding about the meaning of *authentic learning experiences,* **then** teachers will develop a more consistent method of engaging students authentically.

Now it's your turn:

Theory of Action

If . . . (Action),

Then . . . (Outcome).

Guiding Question#1: How are students and teachers working together to create authentic learning experiences?

Sample Problem Framed:

Purpose Statement:

Possible Inquiry Question(s):

If . . .

Then . . .

Activity 12.2 Theory of Action
Supporting Students and Teachers

Example:

Theory of Action

If . . . (Action),

Then . . . (Outcome).

Guiding Question #2: How do we support students and teachers in this process?

Sample Problem Framed: We offer opportunities for teachers to attend professional development but are not sure that the professional development they attend has an impact on teacher and student practices in the classroom.

Purpose Statement: The purpose of this inquiry is to explore more impactful professional learning and development practices that will have a deeper impact on teaching and learning in classrooms.

Possible Inquiry Question(s):

1. What professional learning and development experiences can we create as a school community to support students and teachers in their development around authentic learning experiences?

Evidence: *If* we gain an understanding of the needs of staff when it comes to student learning, *then* we can develop professional learning and development to help meet their needs.

Now it's your turn:

Theory of Action

If . . . (Action),

Then . . . (Outcome).

Guiding Question #2: How do we support students and teachers in this process?

Sample Problem Framed:

Purpose Statement:

Possible Inquiry Question(s):

If . . .

Then . . .

Activity 12.3 Theory of Action
Engaging Families

Example:

Theory of Action

If . . . (Action),

Then . . . (Outcome).

Guiding Question #3: How do we engage families in the process?

Sample Problem Framed: When looking at our communication as a school, we spend more time talking *at* families than we do talking *with* them.

Purpose Statement: The purpose of this inquiry is to develop better strategies to engage families in dialogue around student learning.

Possible Inquiry Question(s):

1.   In what ways do we engage families in discussions that focus on what and how their children learn?

Evidence.

If we can engage families in deeper dialogue through our communication with them, **then** those families will feel less like we are merely communicating at them.

Now it's your turn:

Theory of Action

If . . . (Action).

Then . . . (Outcome).

Guiding Question #3: How do we engage families in the process?

Sample Problem Framed:

Purpose Statement:

Possible Inquiry Question(s):

If . . .

Then . . .

PROGRAM LOGIC MODELS

Now that your team has practiced and possibly even established the focuses for your improvement with the three guiding questions, we will use a program logic model to do the work. I first began using program logic models in *Instructional Leadership* (DeWitt, 2020a). It has been used at both the meso and macro levels in schools. Before we look at the program logic model I created here, I would like to briefly provide some research on program logic models themselves. Renger and Titcomb (2002, p. 493) write, "Developing a logic model is an essential first step in program evaluation." We often jump into a new initiative without thinking clearly about how it may impact people or whether it will have an impact at all. It is important that teams take time to understand exactly where they need to begin so they can develop a common language and common understanding around the improvement.

Program logic models encourage ILTs to think about their present reality and inspire them to begin talking about how they can improve in that area. A logic model is a visual representation that provides a team with an understanding of where they are and where they need to go when it comes to improvement (Bickman, 1987; Dwyer, 1997; Julian et al., 1995; Renger & Titcomb, 2002).

The program logic model in Figure 12.2 is meant to offer five areas to keep your ILT focused on the work. You will notice that the fourth question, which was used in each of the three inquiry questions and theories of action, will now be an integral part of the program logic model.

THEORY OF ACTION

It is now time to take the four guiding questions and begin engaging in the next steps to create an action plan to accomplish those purpose statements. It begins with the Theory of Action column on your program logic model. When your team takes the blank program logic model template (see Appendix 11) and begins to fill it out, they will take the theories of action that they developed and write them into the first section of the program logic model.

RESOURCES

The theories of action that your team created around the areas of authentic learning experiences, support, engaging families, and

Figure 12.2 Program Logic Model

Theory of Action	Resources	Activities	Timetable	Impact
How are students and teachers working together to create authentic learning experiences?	Resources needed to meet Goal #1	Activity #1: Staff Meeting	When and how will you begin taking actionable steps for each activity?	How will students/teachers benefit?
How do we support students and teachers in that process?	Resources needed to meet Goal #2	Activity #2: Grade-Level/Department meeting		What evidence is your team collecting along the way?
How do we engage families in that process?	Resources needed to meet Goal #3	Activity #3: Learning Walks		
What unbiased evidence do we collect to understand our impact?		Activity #4: Student Council/Advisory		

Source: DeWitt, 2021.

collecting unbiased evidence need to involve a discussion around the resources necessary to help achieve the goals. Robinson et al. (2008) write,

> The [leadership] activity is about securing resources that are aligned with instructional purposes, rather than leadership skill in securing resources per se. Thus, this measure should not be interpreted as an indicator of skill in fundraising, grant writing, or partnering with businesses, as those skills may or may not be applied in ways that serve key instructional purposes. (p. 661)

The ILT needs to understand and then define what resources are necessary to achieve their goals. Some resources necessary to meet goals are how they spend their time (i.e., keeping their ILT meetings focused, using time appropriately at faculty meetings, making time for learning walks, etc.).

Other resources may be researched-based articles (i.e., in a previous chapter, we focused on one team role being that of a researcher). Strategic resourcing may also mean finding models of successful practice (i.e., Who is doing this well already? Can members of the team look to their social media communities to find other schools that are already engaging in these practices?). The reality is that more ILTs need to take time to think about the resources they have and how those are aligned with their school goals.

ACTIVITIES

Activities are the actions individuals and teams engage in on a daily basis. The issue is that many people may not be able to speak to the impact those activities have on students or teachers. As Casey (2014, p. 79) suggests, inquiry as a model "means active, engaged hands-on learning. Inquiry thus implies active creation of meaning, which includes new forms of collaborating and new roles for collaborators." The activities outlined here will help do that.

Use the instructional leadership lens and consider that one of the drivers to develop collective leader efficacy is professional learning and development; with this knowledge, determine which activities provide an element of learning. Robinson et al. (2008) say it is important for both leaders and teachers to engage in this learning when she writes,

> more is involved than just supporting or sponsoring other staff in their learning. The leader participates in the learning as leader,

learner, or both. The contexts for such learning are both formal (staff meetings and professional development) and informal (discussions about specific teaching problems). (p. 663)

As we know, teams have to engage in activities that will help them reach their goals, but teams often engage in many activities, some of which may have little impact.

To the point about activities and impact, the following blog post is a cautionary tale about the improvement process. I was inspired to write it after working with a team of well-meaning directors who were juggling a lot of initiatives and expecting school building leaders to carry them out. When I asked them about impact, they came to an unexpected realization.

Are You Activity Rich and Impact Poor?

by Peter DeWitt (2019a)

As I go through [the program logic] process with building leaders and teams, or district leaders and their teams, there has been a glaring issue that becomes obvious to many people around the table. The individuals around the table are really good at writing down countless activities that they may be completing in their positions, but when it comes to impact, they cannot always define the impact their activities are having.

Let's take walk-throughs as an example. Many leaders do walk-throughs in their schools. Some leaders can clearly define why they do walk-throughs and have a common language and common understanding of walk-throughs with staff. However, there are other leaders who feel pressured to do walk-throughs because they see their friends doing them on social media, or they have been told by a superintendent that they are required to do ten walk-throughs a day. Unfortunately, this ends up having very little positive impact on teachers and students because a walk-through that isn't clearly defined or one that is done out of compliance, does not typically result in a positive experience for people in a school.

Reasons Why We Are Activity Rich and Impact Poor

So why does this happen? Why are some individuals so good at completing activities, but after reflecting, they realize that their activities do not always have an impact? There are many reasons why this happens, and our own childhood learning experiences may have something to do with it. Doesn't it always come back to childhood?

There are three reasons why so many teachers, leaders, and teams find that they are good at completing activities but not as impactful as they would like to be:

Accountability train. Over the years, school staff have been made to jump through many hoops; they have had to complete activities out of compliance, and those activities have not always led to a positive impact.

Professional development. This may seem odd coming from a person who facilitates professional learning and development, but going through the program logic model has been eye-opening. Take this example: One district spent tens of thousands of dollars sending teachers out to a popular collaboration conference every year, but their biggest area of need is that their collaboration time is not impactful. The conference is great, but after sending teachers out to it for ten years, there should be a higher level of impact, yes? Professional learning and development many times is an activity that results in little impact. It's one of the reasons why many of us created a competency-based approach to learning.

Self-esteem. It feels good to complete activities. We can check them off the list and say they are done. However, when we dig deeper and look at the impact, we often find that there isn't one.

This is a very fixable issue for teachers and leaders. To make sure that going through a program logic model is not merely an activity without impact, those going through the process may look to see if they have activities that they can cross off the list because there may be significant overlap in activities. In other cases, individuals believe in the activity and begin looking deeper at why those activities have not led to a greater impact.

Overall, in these times of diminishing resources and high levels of burnout among staff and leaders, it's time for teachers and leaders to use a program logic model to see where they spend their time to make sure they are not activity rich and impact poor. This may also give teachers and leaders an opportunity to de-implement an activity that doesn't have any impact.

To remain focused on impacting student learning, I suggest focusing on these four activities.

ACTIVITIES TO REMAIN FOCUSED ON LEARNING

1. **Faculty/staff meetings.** I began flipping my faculty meetings in 2012. Instead of focusing only on accountability and testing, I let teachers have control by asking them what they wanted to learn about. We began discussing topics such as feedback and evidence-based observations. We wanted to make learning central to our meetings. It was my job to find one article or blog that the staff could read prior to the faculty meeting so they would have some surface level of understanding about the topic before we dove deeper into it together.

   Look at your present faculty meetings and determine whether they focus on tasks that could be emailed or whether they focus on the learning necessary to meet the goals you identified in Activities 12.1-12.3. Leadership teams need to find a balance between both and spend 15 minutes on business tasks and the rest of the meeting time on learning.

2. **Grade-level/department meetings.** This is a place to talk about teachers' knowledge and skill, student engagement, and academically engaging content and focus on how they look specific to each grade-level or content area. It's important to remember that this is also the place where the skills of collective responsibility will come in handy because individuals from the ILT will no doubt be questioned by some of their colleagues in this closed-door, school leader-free environment. Let's take a moment here to engage in some reflection about that very idea of pushback.

REFLECT

Pushback

Discuss as a group what individuals from the ILT will say when colleagues push back on the focus of their grade-level or department meeting. For example, what will be the answer when a colleague asks, "Why is leadership making us do this?"

As an aside, grade-level and department meetings will also be the place where a deficit mindset will enter into the equation and colleagues will blame the student, the parents, or the curriculum. How will individuals on the team address those concerns?

If you're looking for my answer, I always find that answering with facts is the best course of action. The fact is that if students are not understanding content or not engaging in learning, it is not because of the student or the parents, sometimes it's because we as teachers are not very engaging.

1. **Learning walks.** Learning walks, which are sometimes called walk-throughs, are at risk of being a one-sided leadership activity that is done *to* teachers and not *with* them. It's important that teachers always have a voice in the walk-through process and that the focus of walk-throughs is on Guiding Question #1 (authentic learning experiences) and Guiding Question #2 (how the team can support those efforts). Have the focus areas on a learning walk form and keep it as short as possible. Perhaps the authentic learning experiences include the following:

   ## Teacher Clarity

   - Factor 1. Explaining through written and verbal examples
   - Factor 2. Personalizing using multiple examples
   - Factor 3. Task orientation
   - Factor 4. Verbal fluency (providing specific details)
   - Factor 5. Organizing student work (encouraging students to take notes; Bush et al., 1977, pp. 55-56).

   ## Student Engagement

   Students could be observed being engaged in their own learning as they use a metacognitive activity (i.e., outline, KWL chart, etc.) or they are enveloped in a project-based learning assignment. Additionally, choice can be represented when it comes to students being engaged in their own learning. Westman (2018, p. 140) writes, "One of the most impressive and effective examples of giving students choice is when choice is built into the learning environment for students and students consistently have the same variety of choices every day."

   (Continued)

Rigorous Content

Academically challenging content includes learning based on vital standards that are inclusive of diverse perspectives and focus on student growth. It incorporates a balance among factual knowledge, procedural knowledge, conceptual knowledge, and metacognitive knowledge. A phrase that comes to mind is that academically challenging content offers moments of cognitive conflict. Stern et al. (2017, p. 30) write, "We must make it clear to students and ourselves that the goal is growth. Students often think of learning as binary; either I know something, or I don't."

Academically challenging content is meant to engage students in new learning that is connected to prior knowledge and fosters growth within the student's level of thinking. Personally, I find that a challenging curriculum fosters a deeper level of curiosity because I have to walk away from it and take a moment to breathe and process, and then I find myself going back to take a deeper look and figure it out.

It is important that the learning walk form offers a chance for dialogue between the teacher and the school building leader. Too often, I have seen leaders who leave the form behind and the teacher is dismayed that they have to hunt down the leader to try to get a moment to talk about it. If ILTs are going to engage in the three goals of strengthening their instructional core, then they need to engage in activities that spark dialogue and not engage in activities that are based on one-sided dialogue. In Appendix 4, I offer a sample learning walk document.

However, I'd like to offer a cautionary note: Too often, leaders, instructional coaches, and teacher leaders are asked to provide feedback from every learning walk. If learning walks are to be relevant, ILTs need to take time to think about their process. If school building leaders spend less than 10 minutes in a classroom, they should not be expected to provide feedback. There are times that I visited the classroom simply to sit with students and build rapport with them.

2. **Student council.** This whole focus on learning is about students, so ILTs need to find ways to engage students in conversations about their level of engagement or the rigor of the content. Some suggest having students be members of the ILT, and that may work with certain schools, but it will not work with everyone. To find a happy medium here, I suggest using student council or advisory groups as a method for understanding student perspectives.

Advisory groups at the elementary level can be created in a number of ways. As an elementary school principal, we had Kids Club, which was our advisory group. Every staff member had a group of students from kindergarten to fifth grade, and each year as the fifth graders left our school for middle school, we had new kindergarteners who entered into our individual groups. As the students went from grade to grade during their elementary years, they stayed within the same Kids Club group. Kids Club was a place where we talked about bullying and asked students for input on different parts of their school experience. Some staff did not enjoy Kids Club because it was an extra duty for them within their school day (we met on Friday mornings every other week, and I scheduled it before prep time began), so we even had the discussion of whether we should keep Kids Club with the students. They asked that we keep doing it, so we did.

As for student council, department or grade-level chairs who are on the ILT may also have the duty of facilitating the student council, so that creates coherence among all of the different groups within the school. However, if members of the ILT do not facilitate the student council, then members of their constituency do, which highlights the importance of the role of the members of the ILT because they need to provide their constituency with clarity around ILT meetings.

The pressure of offering clarity of ILT goals does not solely fall on the individual teacher leaders and instructional coach, it also falls to the school building leader and assistant principals, which is why an activity such as flipped faculty meetings and a more focused learning walk process is a must. It provides coherence. Fullan and Quinn (2016, p. 1) define *coherence* as, "the shared depth of understanding about the purpose and nature of the work." Coherence requires that the ILT defines its timetable. This leads us to the next section.

TIMETABLE

Robinson et al. (2008, p. 663) found that "leaders in higher performing schools are distinguished from their counterparts in otherwise similar lower performing schools by their personal involvement in planning, coordinating, and evaluating teaching and teachers." I understand that it is a leader's job to evaluate, but I have never liked that word. It seems so one-sided and I want leaders and teachers to be able to work together through defining goals and being collaborative members of ILTs.

What I get most out of Robinson et al.'s work, and through my own research and experience as a school building leader, is that we need to set a timetable (or timeline) to follow through on the activities that we agreed upon. These timetables, which you can find a blank template of in Appendix 6, will bring us closer to achieving our goals set through our theories of action. Besides all of that, we know that people stay in the pre-contemplative state of change for far too long, so setting a timetable will help give groups the push they need to actively engage in the activities they created.

It is really up to the team to dictate how long something should take to begin and end. However, when it comes to these four specific activities, the ILT needs to understand that these are yearlong goals. Do not rush the activities. Take the time to use this as an opportunity to discuss the process and learning, which is the second to last part of the inquiry cycle.

Remember that improvement is a yearlong process in which your ILT and your school community at large should be looking for short-term wins while focusing on long-term gains. These activities are not something to check off a list, they are places where we learn together.

For example, I once worked with a principal who flipped every faculty meeting. Although good intentions were behind it, he would focus on a new instructional strategy at every meeting. In October, he focused on reciprocal teaching, November was the jigsaw method, and December was using a fishbowl activity in the classroom. The problem was that he created initiative fatigue among his staff because he would be on to a new instructional strategy before the staff had the opportunity to try the one from the previous month. I asked him to slow down and offered the following timetable:

October. In October, staff read an article on reciprocal teaching prior to the meeting. During the meeting, they learned what it looks like, and a teacher leader led staff in a reciprocal activity. The staff was then asked to try the same strategy with their students over the next month and perhaps even record themselves using it. Because staff have different levels of understanding, some staff would use the strategy for the first time while others who were much more versed in using it would add a twist or show how it encouraged differentiation.

November. In November, teachers came back to the faculty meeting and spent time discussing the challenges and successes of using reciprocal teaching in their classrooms.

December. In December, staff could focus on a new strategy, but they should take November to discuss the one they learned together in October and celebrate the success of doing it with students.

Whatever the timetable that is decided upon, try to think about mindset (Chapter 2 of this book) as well as well-being (Chapter 3) and slow things down. Appendix 6 offers an example of a checklist that could be used as a timetable. Please remember, checklists are used as a way to keep track of progress, but they need to be used as a catalyst for deep learning among staff. Don't simply check something off the list; engage in the activity with depth.

IMPACT

Last but not least is impact. How will teams make sure they are not activity rich and impact poor? The program logic model is meant to create a level of coherence and to spur reflection among the team and staff. As Casey and Bruce (2011, p. 79) suggest, "Reflection means expressing experience, and thereby being able to move from new concepts into action. Reflection may also mean recognising further indeterminacies, leading to continuing inquiry." ILTs need to collect evidence to understand this part of the inquiry process. Ward et al. (2013, p. 1) state, "The problem is not that some schools have access to information and others do not. Schools are awash in information about most aspects of their operation. Some schools just choose to ignore the information that is available to them." I often wonder if it's another issue as well when it comes to data and evidence. If schools are awash with data, perhaps it's also that they have too much data and do not know where to begin.

The bottom line here is to understand what evidence to collect, and that is where collective leader efficacy can definitely be fostered. The best possible evidence an ILT can collect is the evidence they decide upon together. I write that because many years ago, I reached out to an assessment researcher and friend, Tom Guskey. I asked Tom to explain self-efficacy to me because it seems too easy. All we have to do is raise the confidence of teachers and BOOM! Efficacy is raised. Guskey responded that it's not that easy (personal communication, May 17, 2017. The bold print is Guskey's and the rest is my commentary on each point). There are three necessary components of raising the self-efficacy of individuals:

1. **Protocol in place.** This is why I refer back to faculty meetings, grade-level/department meetings, learning walks, and student councils. These are protocols that most schools have in place.

2. **Evidence of teachers' trust.** Many of us who have spent a number of years as teachers and/or leaders understand how accountability measures did not build a lot of trust. What individuals and teams need is some level of autonomy so they can collect valid and reliable evidence that they trust.

3. **See improvement within weeks and not months.** We need instant gratification. We even binge-watch shows now because we can't wait from one week to the next to see the show. That being said, it's important that we do see improvement in the way teachers talk with one another and how students engage in their own learning within their classrooms.

It's similar to success criteria in student learning. The most impactful success criteria are the kind that is developed between students and teachers, so the same can be said here. The best evidence is what your team decides together. Keep in mind that each member of the team can discuss this process with the grade level or department they represent and bring those ideas back to the ILT meeting. To do that, the team needs to look at the following questions:

▶ What is our goal?

▶ If we could paint a picture of what that goal looks like in the classroom, how would we describe that picture?

▶ What formative assessment tools are teachers using in those classrooms that can also be used as evidence of learning?

In Appendix 10, I offer templates that can be used to understand and collect evidence of impact.

IN THE END

In order for ILTs to reach their full potential and create collective leader efficacy together, they must engage in goal setting that will have a positive impact on the school community. Remember that in Chapter 1 of this book, we focused on Fullan's (2011) research around drivers; he stated that a driver had to do the following:

1. foster intrinsic motivation of teachers and students,

2. engage educators and students in continuous improvement of instruction and learning,

3. inspire collective or teamwork, [and]

4. affect all teachers and students—100 percent. (p. 3)

We have used four guiding questions to focus the efforts of your ILT. Three of the four questions were used to develop purpose statements, inquiry questions, and theories of action. We began this chapter with that theory of action process and then were introduced to the program logic model. Using a program logic model helps teams process what their goals should look like, what resources they will need to achieve them, and what activities they should engage in to move forward with staff and create a deeper understanding. Teams need to hold themselves accountable by creating a timetable and then collect evidence to understand impact. The last thing an ILT would want is to be activity rich and impact poor, because that does not build collective leader efficacy.

The goal of this book was to guide teams through the process of coming together, understand the research behind instructional leadership, and go through a cycle of inquiry that will ultimately impact students for the better as the team develops collective leader efficacy together. Collective leader efficacy is the shared conviction that a school's ILT can make a significant contribution in raising student achievement. Did this help your team not only engage in joint work but also develop a shared conviction together?

I wrote this book as if I were facilitating a competency-based workshop in which your teams were engaged in a project-based learning mentality as you learned from one another; you may have tried activities that worked and some that did not. If you remember, at the beginning of this book, we focused on how schools act as systems when they develop processes that help them learn and adapt as they work together to be a learning organization. The book was meant to help your team and your school community become a learning organization.

Lastly, I want to thank you for reading this book individually or as a collective. Even if we did not talk with each other during the reading of the book (although it would be great if we could!), I always appreciate it when someone takes the time to read and engage in the work that I developed through research and practice.

Thank you.

Peter DeWitt, EdD

GUIDING QUESTIONS

- Why is it important for an instructional leadership team to process what improvement initiatives look like?
- When research says *strategic resourcing*, what does that mean?
- Why are some schools activity rich and impact poor?
- Why does an instructional leadership team need to develop a timetable?
- Why is it that some schools are awash with data but do very little with that data?
- Where does evidence fit into your instructional leadership team's improvement process?

What two questions do you wish I had asked?

1.

2.

What three new areas of learning did you experience while reading this chapter?

1.

2.

3.

NOTES

APPENDICES

APPENDIX 1

Instructional Leadership Team (ILT) Request for Inclusion on the Team

Thank you for your interest in being a member of our instructional leadership team. We work together as a group, challenge each other's thinking and try to go deep with our learning. We value the time you take answering the questions and providing some questions of your own.

Name
Department/Grade Level
If you have been a part of other instructional leadership teams, what is one quality that you bring to the table?
If this is your first instructional leadership team, please tell us a bit about what you can bring to the table.

(Continued)

(Continued)

Name
Department/Grade Level
Tell us about a time that you challenged the thinking of your colleagues. Why did you challenge them? How did you go about offering the challenge? How did it all work out in the end?
Let's take that last question a bit further. How do you feel about challenging the thinking of your school leader(s)? Have you done that before? What did that conversation look like if you did challenge your school leader in the past?
When our team engages in a model of inquiry, what areas do you think we should look at?
What are some questions you have for us? What do you wish we had asked that we didn't?

APPENDIX 2

Activity: Cultivating Mindsets of Collaboration

- ❯ Place these eight phrases on sticky notes.

- ❯ In a breakout group, discuss how these 8 phrases are interrelated.

- ❯ Provide up to 10 minutes for this activity.

- ❯ Have each group build a visual representation.

- ❯ **Focus for discussion:**

    School Leadership Team

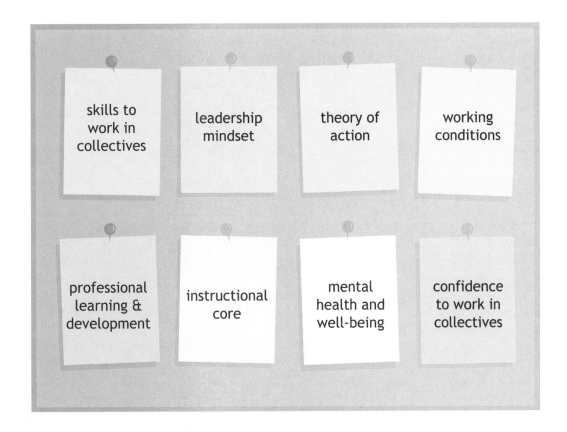

APPENDIX 3

Weekly Log: Where Do You Spend Your Time?

Using this form, track where you spend your time for one week. If this is to work, you must be honest. Don't judge yourself for not doing what you think you should be doing. Just simply track where you spend your efforts.

This is the week of (date) _____.

Monday Month, day, year
Tuesday Month, day, year
Wednesday Month, day, year
Thursday Month, day, year
Friday Month, day, year

APPENDIX 4

Learning Walk Form

This form will be used for learning walks that last for a duration of 10 minutes or more. There is one area of focus— how students and teachers are engaged in authentic learning experiences (i.e., learning intentions, success criteria and teacher clarity). Are learning intentions and success criteria evident? How has teacher clarity been accomplished?

Learning intentions were available to students through a visible or verbal method.
☐ Evident
☐ Somewhat evident
☐ Not evident at all
☐ N/A
The following is the evidence gathered to support whether learning intentions were evident or not.
Success criteria were evident during instruction.
☐ Evident
☐ Somewhat evident
☐ Not evident at all
☐ N/A
The following is a factual example of how success criteria were evident (or not) during instruction.

(Continued)

(Continued)

Instruction included the following elements of teacher clarity.

☐ Factor 1. Explaining through written and verbal examples

☐ Factor 2. Personalizing using multiple examples

☐ Factor 3. Task orientation

☐ Factor 4. Verbal fluency (providing specific details)

☐ Factor 5. Organizing student work (encouraging students to take notes)

The following is a factual example of how teacher clarity was evident (or not) during instruction.

Students were engaged in learning in one of the following ways:

☐ Direct instruction

☐ Metacognitive activity (creating an outline for an assignment; engaging in a KWL chart)

☐ Project-based learning

☐ Student choice (students can consistently choose from a list of activities)

Teacher response and feedback to learning walk.

How did this lesson create an authentic learning experience for students?

What evidence are we collecting to understand our impact?

APPENDIX 5

Guiding Questions 1–4

With your instructional leadership team, engage in open dialogue about these questions. It does not mean that the team only focuses on what they are not doing. Make sure the team focuses on the positive experiences for students in the school. Additionally, this form can be shared with grade levels and departments or with student council so those groups can explore them as well.

How are students and teachers working together to create authentic learning experiences?
What does the term "authentic learning experiences" mean to your instructional leadership team?

(Continued)

(Continued)

What are some academic examples of those experiences?

What are some social-emotional examples of those experiences?

APPENDIX 6

Timetable Checklist

The instructional leadership team (ILT) will decide when the timetable will begin for each of the activities defined in the program logic model. The following is an example of what that could look like.

Faculty Meeting (September)

☐ Staff discuss the process of flipping faculty meetings

☐ October focus: authentic learning experiences

☐ Four days before October faculty meeting: article on student engagement will be sent out

☐ Teachers read it on their own and bring their best example of engagement to October meeting

☐ School building leader shares learning walk form and asks for input

Grade-level/department meeting

☐ ILT leader shares purpose of flipped faculty meeting

☐ Grade level/department engages about three ILT areas of focus

☐ Grade level/department discusses these goals as being the focus of learning walks

☐ Grade level/department discusses learning walk form

☐ Other:

(Continued)

(Continued)

Learning Walks

☐ Learning walks begin in October

☐ Focus: authentic learning; support; engaging families

☐ Forms will only be used for observations longer than 10 minutes

☐ Forms are used for dialogue and no compliance

☐ Forms are used to foster a culture of feedback

Student council/advisory board (October)

☐ Student council leader discusses three goals of the school

☐ Student council considers creating a survey on Google for students

☐ Student council sees a copy of learning walk form

☐ Student council talks about the role of feedback in teaching and learning

---

APPENDIX 7

Purpose Statements 1-3

PURPOSE STATEMENT 1

Guiding Question #1

How do students and teachers engage in authentic learning experiences?

SAMPLE

Problem Framed: In walk-throughs and formal observations, we notice that many students are engaged in surface-level work. We want students to experience deeper learning.

Purpose Statement: The purpose of this inquiry is to discover how often our students and teachers engage in deep and transfer-level learning.

YOUR TEAM'S TURN

Problem Framed:

Purpose Statement:

PURPOSE STATEMENT 2
Guiding Question #2

How do we support students and teachers in this process?

Sample Problem Framed: We offer opportunities for teachers to attend professional development but are not sure that the professional development they attend has an impact on teacher and student practices in the classroom.

Purpose Statement: The purpose of this inquiry is to explore more impactful professional learning and development practices that will have a deeper impact on teaching and learning in classrooms.

YOUR TEAM'S TURN

Problem Framed:

Purpose Statement:

PURPOSE STATEMENT 3
Guiding Question #3

How do we engage families in this process?

Sample Problem Framed: When looking at our communication as a school, we spend more time talking *at* families than we do talking *with* them.

Purpose Statement: The purpose of this inquiry is to develop better strategies to engage families in dialogue around student learning.

YOUR TEAM'S TURN

Problem Framed:

Purpose Statement:

APPENDIX 8

Inquiry Questions 1-3

INQUIRY QUESTION 1
Guiding Question #1

Authentic learning experiences

SAMPLE

Possible Inquiry Questions: How do teachers, leaders, and students define deep and transfer-level learning experiences?

Possible Evidence: What evidence can we collect to help us gain that understanding.

YOUR TEAM'S TURN

Possible Inquiry Questions:

Possible Evidence:

INQUIRY QUESTION 2
Guiding Question #2

How do we support students and teachers in the process?

Possible Inquiry Questions: What professional learning and development experiences can we create as a school community to support students and teachers in their development around authentic learning experiences?

Possible Evidence:

YOUR TEAM'S TURN

Possible Inquiry Questions:

Possible Evidence:

INQUIRY QUESTION 3
Guiding Question #3

How do we engage families in this process?

Possible Inquiry Questions: In what ways do we engage families in discussions that focus on what and how their children learn?

Possible Evidence:

YOUR TEAM'S TURN

Possible Inquiry Questions:

Possible Evidence:

APPENDIX 9

Theory of Action

Sample:

If . . . (Action),

Then . . . (Outcome).

Guiding Question #1: How do students and teachers engage in authentic learning experiences?

Sample Problem Framed: In walk-throughs and formal observations, we notice that many students are engaged in surface-level work. We want students to experience deeper learning.

Purpose Statement: The purpose of this inquiry is to discover how often our students and teachers engage in deep and transfer-level learning.

Possible Inquiry Questions: How do teachers, leaders, and students define deep and transfer-level learning experiences?

Evidence: What evidence can we collect to help us gain that understanding?

If we can develop a common language and common understanding about what authentic learning experiences means, *then* teachers will develop a more consistent method of engaging students authentically.

(Continued)

(Continued)

Template:

If . . . (Action),

Then . . . (Outcome).

Guiding Question:

Sample Problem Framed:

Purpose Statement:

Possible Inquiry Questions:

Evidence:

If . . .

then . . .

APPENDIX 10

Theory of Action Evidence Template

Theory of Action Evidence #1

How are students and teachers engaged in authentic learning experiences?	Evidence Artifact
Leadership Action: Learning walk, formal observation	
Teacher Action: Project-based learning, classroom assessment, teacher observation	
Student Action: Portfolio, student-led conference, artifact chosen by student	

Theory of Action Evidence #2

How do we support students and teachers in that process?	Evidence Artifact
Leadership Action: Learning walk, formal observation	
Teacher Action: Project-based learning, classroom assessment, teacher observation	
Student Action: Portfolio, student-led conference, artifact chosen by student	

Theory of Action Evidence #3

How do we engage families in that process?	Evidence Artifact
Leadership Action: Learning walk, formal observation	
Teacher Action: Project-based learning, classroom assessment, teacher observation	
Student Action: Portfolio, student-led conference, artifact chosen by student	

APPENDIX 11

Blank Template Program Logic Model

Program Logic Model

Theory of Action	Resources	Activities	Timetable	Impact

Source: **DeWitt, 2021.**

REFERENCES

Anderson, N. J., Bachman, L., Perkins, K., & Cohen, A. (1991). An exploratory study into the construct validity of a reading comprehension test: Triangulation of data sources. *Language Testing, 8*(1), 41–66.

Association of Directors of Education in Scotland (ADES). (2017). *Towards a learning system: A new approach to raising standards for all in Scottish school*s. The Staff College.

Baba, T. (2019). The importance of intellectually safe classrooms for our Keiki. *Educational Perspectives, 51*(1), 28–30.

Bandura, A. (1997). *Self-efficacy: The exercise of control*. Freeman.

Bandura, A. (2000). Cultivate self-efficacy for personal and organizational effectiveness. In E. A. Locke (Ed.), *The Blackwell handbook of principles of organizational behaviour* (pp. 120–136). Blackwell.

Bandura, A. (2005). *Self-efficacy. Beliefs of adolescents*. Information Age Publishing.

Barnett, K., & McCormick, J. (2012). Leadership and team dynamics in senior executive leadership teams. *Educational Management Administration & Leadership, 40*(6), 653–671. https://doi.org/10.1177/1741143212456909

Bickman, L. (1987). The functions of program theory. In L. Bickman (Ed.), *Using program theory in evaluation. New directions for program evaluation, no. 33.* Jossey-Bass.

Boser, U., Wilhelm, M., & Hanna, R. (2014, October 6). *The power of the Pygmalion effect teachers expectations strongly predict college completion.* Center for American Progress. https://www.americanprogress.org/issues/education-k-12/reports/2014/10/06/96806/the-power-of-the-pygmalion-effect/

Boston Consulting Group. (2014). *Teachers know best: Teachers' views on professional development*. Bill & Melinda Gates Foundation.

Brackett, M. (2019). *Permission to feel. Unlocking the power of emotions to help our kids, ourselves, and our society thrive*. Celadon Books.

Brackett, M., Cannizzarro, M., & Levy, S. (2020). The pandemic's toll on school leaders is palpable. Here's what's needed for a successful school year. *Ed Surge.* https://www.edsurge.com/news/2020-07-16-the-pandemic-s-toll-on-school-leaders-is-palpable-here-s-what-s-needed-for-a-successful-school-year

Burke, S., Stagl, K., & Klein, C. (2006). What types of leadership behaviour are functional in teams? A meta-analysis. *Leadership Quarterly, 17*(3), 288–307.

Burkhauser, S. (2017). How much do school principals matter when it comes to teacher working conditions? *Educational Evaluation and Policy Analysis, 39*(1), 126–145. https://doi.org/10.3102/0162373716668028

Bush, A. J., Kennedy, J. J., & Cruickshank, D. R. (1977). An empirical investigation of teacher clarity. *Journal of Teacher Education, 28*(2), 53–58.

Cambridge Dictionary. (2021). Confidence. *Cambridge dictionary.* https://dictionary.cambridge.org/us/dictionary/english/confidence

Campbell, C., Osmond-Johnson, P., Faubert, B., Zeichner, K., & Hobbs-Johnson, A. (with Brown, S., DaCosta, P., Hales, A., Kuehn, L., Sohn, J., & Steffensen, K.). (2017). *The state of educators' professional learning in Canada.* Learning Forward.

Casey L. (2014). *Questions, curiosity and the inquiry cycle.* E-Learning and Digital Media.

Casey, L., & Bruce, B. C. (2011). The practice profile of inquiry: Connecting digital literacy and pedagogy. *E-Learning and Digital Media, 8*(1), 76–85. https://www.ideals.illinois.edu/bitstream/handle/2142/18755/The%20Practice%20Profile%20of%20Inquiry%20-%20Connecting%20Digital%20Literacy%20and%20Pedagogy%20%28Postprint%29.pdf?sequence=2&isAllowed=y

Cliffe, J., Fuller, K., & Moorosi, P. (2018). Secondary school leadership preparation and development: Experiences and aspirations of members of senior leadership teams. *Management in Education, 32*(2), 85–91. https://doi.org/10.1177/0892020618762714

Costanza, J. F., Tracy, Saundra, J., & Holmes, R. (1987). Expanding Instructional Leadership Through Department Chair. *NASSP Bulletin, 71*(502), 77–82.

Czarnec, J., & Hill, M. (2018). Schemata and instructional strategies. *The Evolution.* https://evolllution.com/programming/teaching-and-learning/schemata-and-instructional-strategies/

Datnow, A., & Park, V. (2018). *Professional collaboration with purpose: Teacher learning towards equitable and excellent schools.* Routledge.

Davis, L. P., & Museus, S. D. (2019, July 19). *Identifying and disrupting deficit thinking.* National Center for Institutional Diversity. https://medium.com/national-center-for-institutional-diversity/identifying-and-disrupting-deficit-thinking-cbc6da326995

Department of Education of Western Australia. (2018). *Western Australian public school leadership strategy 2018-2021.* Department of Education of Western Australia.

Dewey, J. (1956). *The child and the curriculum & The school and society.* University of Chicago Press. (Original works published 1902 and 1915).

DeWitt, P. (2019a). Are you activity rich and impact poor? Finding Common Ground. *Education Week.*

DeWitt, P. (2019b). *Coach it further. Using the art of coaching to improve school leadership.* Corwin Press.

DeWitt, P. (2020a). *Instructional leadership: Creating practice out of theory.* Corwin Press.

DeWitt, P. (2020b, October 4). How team walk-throughs can engage educators in remote learning. Finding Common Ground. *Education Week.* https://www.edweek.org/education/opinion-how-team-walk-throughs-can-engage-educators-in-remote-learning/2020/10

DeWitt, P. (2020c, October 24). School leaders were asked about their stress levels. Here's what they told us. Finding Common Ground. *Education Week.*

Dimmock, C. (2016). System leadership for school improvement: A developing concept and set of practices, *Scottish Educational Review, 48*(2), 60–79.

Dimmock, C., & Walker, A. (2002). School leadership in context: Societal and organisational cultures. In T. Bush, & L. Bell (Eds.), *The principles and practice of educational management* (pp. 70-85). Series: Educational Management, Research and Practice. Paul Chapman Publishing.

Dinham, S., Ingvarson, L. C., & Kleinhenz, E. (2008). *Teaching talent: The best teachers for Australia's classrooms.*

Donohoo, J. (2013). *Collaborative inquiry for educators. A facilitator's guide to school improvement.* Corwin Press.

Donohoo, J. (2017). *Collective efficacy. How educators' beliefs impact student learning.* Corwin Press.

Donohoo, J., & Mausbach, A. (2021). Beyond collaboration: The power of joint work. *Educational Leadership, 78*(5), 22-26.

Doyle, W. (1983). Academic work. *Review of Educational Research, 53*(2), 159-199. https://doi.org/10.3102/00346543053002159

Dufour, R. (2002, May). The learning-centered principal. *Educational Leadership, 59*(8). Beyond Instructional Leadership, 12-15.

Dweck, C. (2006). *Mindset: The new psychology of success.* Random House.

Dweck, C. (2015, September 22). Carol Dweck revisits the 'growth mindset.' *Education Week.*

Dwyer, J. (1997). Using a program logic model that focuses on performance measurement to develop a program. *Canadian Journal of Public Health, 88*(6), 421-425.

Education Week Research Center. (2019). *Principals. Here's how teachers view you.* Education Week.

Edmonds, R. (1979). Effective schools for the urban poor. *Educational Leadership, 37*, 15-24.

Elmore, R. (2006). Breaking the cartel. *Phi Delta Kappan, 87*(7), 517-518.

Elmore, R. (2009). *Instructional rounds in education: A network approach to improving teaching and learning.* Harvard Education Press.

Firestone, W. A., & Pennell, J. R. (1993). Teacher commitment, working conditions, and differential incentive policies. *Review of Educational Research, 63*(4), 489-525. https://doi.org/10.3102/00346543063004489

Firestone, W. A., & Rosenblum, S. (1988). Building Commitment in Urban High Schools. *Educational Evaluation and Policy Analysis, 10*(4), 285-299. https://doi.org/10.3102/01623737010004285

Fisher, D., Frey, N., & Hattie, J. (2016). *Visible learning for literacy. Implementing the practices that work best to accelerate student learning.* Corwin Press.

Ford, T. G., Lavigne, A. L., Fiegener, A. M., & Si, S. (2020). Understanding district support for leader development and success in the accountability era: A review of the literature using social-cognitive theories of motivation. *Review of Educational Research, 90*(2), 264-307. https://doi.org/10.3102/0034654319899723

Forde, C., & Torrance, D. (2017). Social justice and leadership development. *Professional Development in Education, 43*(1), 106-120.

Fredricks, J. A., Blumenfeld, P. C., & Paris, A. H. (2004). School engagement: Potential of the concept, state of the evidence. *Review of Educational Research, 74*(1), 59-109. https://doi.org/10.3102/00346543074001059

Fullan, M. (2011, May). *Choosing the wrong drivers for whole system reform.* Centre for Strategic Education Seminar Series Paper No. 204. Centre for Strategic Education.

Fullan, M. (2017). *Indelible leadership. Always leave them learning.* Corwin Press.

Fullan, M., & Hargreaves, A. (2017). Call to action: Bringing the profession back in. *Learning Forward.*

Fullan, M., & Quinn, J. (2016). *Coherence. The right drivers in action for schools, districts and systems.* Corwin Press.

Fuller, E. J., Young, M. D., Richardson, M. S., Pendola, A., & Kathleen, M. W. (2018). *The PreK-8 school leader in 2018 A 10-year study.* NAESP.

General Teaching Council for Scotland. (2021). *Professional standards 2021*. GTC Scotland. https://www.gtcs.org.uk/professional-standards/professional-standards-2021-engagement.aspx

Gobir, N. (2020). 'Every Kid is Motivated': Action-oriented ideas to revive students' curiosity. *Mindshift*. https://www.kqed.org/mindshift/57152/every-kid-is-motivated-action-oriented-ideas-to-revive-students-curiosity

Goddard, R. D., Hoy, W. K., & Hoy, A. W. (2000). Collective teacher efficacy: Its meaning, measure, and impact on student achievement. *American Educational Research Journal, 37*(2), 479-507.

Goddard, R. D., Hoy, W. K., & Hoy, A. W. (2004). Collective efficacy beliefs: Theoretical developments, empirical evidence, and future directions. *Educational Researcher, 33*(3), 3-13.

Goleman, D., & Boyatzis, R. E. (2017). Emotional intelligence has 12 elements. Which do you need to work on? *Harvard Business Review*. https://hbr.org/2017/02/emotional-intelligence-has-12-elements-which-do-you-need-to-work-on

Greenleaf, R. K. (1977). *Servant leadership. A journey into the nature of legitimate power and greatness*. Paulist Press.

Guskey, T. (2021). Professional learning with staying power. Six steps to evidence-based professional learning that makes a difference. *Educational Leadership, 78*(5), 54-60.

Hannigan, J., & Hannigan, J. (2016). *Don't suspend me! An alternative discipline toolkit*. Corwin Press.

Hargreaves, A., & Fullan, M. (2012). *Professional capital. Transforming teaching in every school*. Teachers College Press.

Hargreaves, A., & O'Connor, M. T. (2018a). *Collaborative professionalism: When teaching together means learning for all*. Corwin Press.

Hargreaves, A., & O'Connor, M. T. (2018b). Solidarity with solidity: The case for collaborative professionalism. *Phi Delta Kappan, 100*(1), 20-24.

Hargreaves, A., & Shirley, D. (2012). *The global fourth way. The quest for educational excellence*. Corwin Press.

Harris, A. (2011). System improvement through collective capacity building. *Journal of Educational Administration, 49*(6), 624-636.

Harris, A. (2013). Distributed leadership: Friend or foe? *Educational Management Administration & Leadership, 41*(5), 545-554. https://doi.org/10.1177/1741143213497635

Harvard Medical School. (2018, August). *Protect your brain from stress. Stress management may reduce health problems linked to stress, which include cognitive problems and a higher risk for Alzheimer's disease and dementia*. https://www.health.harvard.edu/mind-and-mood/protect-your-brain-from-stress

Hattie, J. (2012). *Visible learning for teachers. Maximizing impact on learning*. Routledge.

Hattie, J. (2014). *Hattie effect size list—195 influences related to achievement*. https://visible-learning.org/hattie-ranking-influences-effect-sizes-learning

Hattie, J. (2016). Third annual visible learning conference (subtitled "Mindframes and Maximizers"). Washington, DC, July 11, 2016.

Hattie, J., Donohoo, J., & DeWitt, P. (2020). Understanding impact to foster collective efficacy. *Principal Connections. Ontario Principal's Association, 24*(2), 15-17.

Hattie, J., Fisher, D., Frey, N., & Clarke, S. (2021). *Collective student efficacy: Developing independent and interdependent learners*. Corwin Press.

Hattie, J., & Yates, C. R. (2014). *Visible learning and the science of how we learn.* Routledge.

Headlee, C. (2015). 10 ways to have a better conversation. *Ted Talks.* https://www.ted.com/talks/celeste_headlee_10_ways_to_have_a_better_conversation

Heale, R., & Forbes, D. (2013). Understanding triangulation in research. *Evidence-Based Nursing, 16*(4), 98.

Hoy, W. K., Tarter, C. J., & Bliss, J. R. (1990). Organizational climate, school health, and effectiveness: A comparative analysis. *Educational Administration Quarterly, 26*(3), 260-279.

Hulpia, H., Devos, G., & Van Keer, H. (2011). The relation between school leadership from a distributed perspective and teachers' organizational commitment: Examining the source of the leadership function. *Educational Administration Quarterly, 47*(5), 728-771.

Institute for Health and Human Potential. (2019). *The meaning of emotional intelligence.* https://www.ihhp.com/meaning-of-emotional-intelligence/

International Labor Organization. (2015). *Working conditions.* http://www.ilo.org/global/topics/working-conditions/lang--en/index.htm

Johnson, S. M. (2006). *The workplace matters: Teacher quality, retention and effectiveness* (NEA Best Practices Working Paper). NEA.

Julian, D. A., Jones, A., & Deyo, D. (1995). Open systems evaluation and the logic model: Program planning and evaluation tools. *Evaluation and Program Planning, 18*(4), 333-341.

Kavanagh, J., & Rich, M. D. (2018). *Truth decay: An initial exploration of the diminishing role of facts and analysis in American public life.* RAND Corporation. https://www.rand.org/pubs/research_reports/RR2314.html. Also available in print form.

Kennedy, F., Carroll, B., Francoeur, J. (2013). Mindset not skill set: Evaluating in new paradigms of leadership development. *Advances in Developing Human Resources, 15*(1), 10-26.

Klocko, B. A., & Wells, C. M. (2015). Workload pressures of principals: A focus on renewal, support, and mindfulness. *NASSP Bulletin, 99*(4), 332-355. https://doi.org/10.1177/0192636515619727

Knight, J. (2016). *Better conversations. Coaching ourselves and each other to be more credible, caring and connected.* Corwin Press.

Koh, W. L., Steers, R. M., & Terborg, J. R. (1995). The effects of transformational leadership on teacher attitudes and student performance in Singapore. *Journal of Organizational Behavior, 16*(4), 319-333.

Kress, G., & van Leeuwen, T. (2001). *Multimodal discourse: The modes and media of contemporary communication.* Bloomsbury.

Ladd, H. F. (2011). Teachers' Perceptions of their working conditions: How predictive of planned and actual teacher movement? *Educational Evaluation and Policy Analysis, 33*(2), 235-261. https://doi.org/10.3102/0162373711398128

LaMorte, W. (2019). *The social cognitive theory.* Boston University School of Public Health. https://sphweb.bumc.bu.edu/otlt/mph-Chapters/sb/behavioralchangetheories/behavioralchangetheories5.html

Le Fevre, D., Timperley, H., Twyford, K., & Ell, F. (2020). *Leading powerful professional learning. Responding to complexity with adaptive expertise.* Corwin Press.

Leithwood, K., & Jantzi, D. (2008, October). Linking leadership to student learning: The contributions of leader efficacy. *Educational Administration Quarterly, 44*(4), 496-528.

Leithwood, K., & Mascall, B. (2008, October). Collective leadership effects on student achievement. *Educational Administration Quarterly, 44*(4), 529-561. https://doi.org/10.1177/0013161X08321221

Lencioni, P. (2002). *Five dysfunctions of a team. A leadership fable.* Jossey-Bass.

Levin, S., Leung, M., Edgerton, A., & Scott, C. (2020). Elementary school principals' professional learning: Current status and future needs. *Learning Policy Institute.* National Association of Elementary School Principals. https://learningpolicyinstitute.org/sites/default/files/product-files/NAESP_Elementary_Principals_Professional_Learning_BRIEF.pdf

Levine, A. (2005). *Educating school leaders.* The Education Schools Project.

Lew, M. (2020, October 30). Creative approaches to supporting the emotional well-being of staff three strategies school leaders can implement to help ensure that all staff members manage the stresses of this year. *Edutopia.*

Mahfouz, J., Greenberg, M. T., & Rodriguez, A. (2019). *Principals' social and emotional competence: A key factor for creating caring schools.* Penn State University Research Brief.

Maslow, A. H. (1968). *Toward a psychology of being.* Van Nostrand.

Mayo Clinic. (2020). *Depression. Major depressive disorder.*https://www.mayoclinic.org/diseases-conditions/depression/symptoms-causes/syc-20356007

McCormick, M. J. (2001). Self-efficacy and leadership effectiveness: Applying social cognitive theory to leadership. *Journal of Leadership Studies, 8*(1), 22-33.

Miller, P. (2018). 'Culture,' 'context,' school leadership and entrepreneurialism: Evidence from sixteen countries. *Education Sciences, 8*(2), 76.

Mitani, H. (2018). Principals' working conditions, job stress, and turnover behaviors under NCLB accountability pressure. *Educational Administration Quarterly, 54*(5), 822-862.

Mitchell, A. (2019). *Professional collaboration to improve educational outcomes in Scottish schools: Developing a conceptual framework.* [Unpublished dissertation]. School of Education, University of Glasgow.

Morrow, P. C. (1993). *The theory and measurement of work commitment.* JAI Press.

Mowday, R., Steers, R., & Porter, L. (1979). The measurement of organizational commitment. *Journal of Vocational Behavior, 14*(2), 224-247.

Mutz, D., & Mondak, J. (2006). The workplace as a context for cross-cutting political discourse. *The Journal of Politics, 68*(1), 140-155.

National Association of Secondary School Principals (NASSP). (2020). *With nearly half of principals considering leaving, research urges attention to working conditions, compensation, and supports.* https://www.nassp.org/news/with-nearly-half-of-principals-considering-leaving-research-urges-attention-to-working-conditions-compensation-and-supports/#:~:text=Concerns%20about%20principal%20turnover%20are,poverty%20schools%20and%20rural%20communities

New South Wales Department of Education. (September 2017). *Principal workload and time use study.* New South Wales Department of Education.

Nguni, S., Sleegers, P., & Denessen, E. (2006). Transformational and transactional leadership effects on teachers' job satisfaction, organizational commitment, and organizational citizenship behavior in primary schools: The Tanzanian case. *School Effectiveness and School Improvement, 17*(2), 145-177.

Nuthall, G. (2007). *The hidden lives of learners.* NZCER Press.

Odetola, T. O., Erickson, E. L., Bryan, C. E., & Walker, L. (1972). Organizational structure and student alienation. *Educational Administration Quarterly, 8*(1), 15-26.

Perry, A. (2020). *Know your price. Valuing black lives and property in America's black cities.* Brookings Institute Press.

Pickett, C. L. Gardner, W. L., & Knowles, M. (2004). Getting a cue: The need to belong and enhanced sensitivity to social cues. *Personality and Social Psychology Bulletin, 30*(9), 1095-1107.

Pijanowski, J. C., & Brady, K. P. (2009). The influence of salary in attracting and retaining school leaders. *Education and Urban Society, 42*(1), 25-41.

Pont, B., Nusche, D., & Moorman, H. (2008). *Improving school leadership Volume 1: Policy and practice.* OECD.

Queen, J. A., & Schumacher, D. (2006). A survival guide for frazzled principals. *Principal Magazine.* NAESP.

Renger, R., & Titcomb, A. A. (2002). Three-step approach to teaching logic models. *American Journal of Evaluation, 23*(4), 493-503.

Rhinesmith, S. H. (1992). Global mindsets for global managers. *Training and Development, Alexandria American Society for Training and Development, 46*(10), 63-69.

Rhinesmith, S. H. (1995). Open door to a global mindset. *Training & Development, 49*(5), 35-43.

Riley, P., See, S-M., Marsh, H., & Dicke, T. (2021). *The Australian Principal Occupational Health, Safety and Wellbeing Survey* (IPPE Report). Sydney: Institute for Positive Psychology and Education, Australian Catholic University.

Ritchhart, R., Church, M., & Morrison, K. (2011). *Making thinking visible: How to promote engagement, understanding, and independence for all learners.* John Wiley and Sons.

Robinson, V. M. J. (2001). Descriptive and normative research on organizational learning: Locating the contribution of Argyris and Schön. *International Journal of Educational Management, 15*(2), 58-67.

Robinson, V. M. J. (2008). Forging the links between distributed leadership and educational outcomes. *Journal of Educational Administration, 46*(2), 241-256.

Robinson, V. M. J. (2018). *Reduce change to increase improvement.* Corwin Impact Leadership Series. Corwin Press.

Robinson, V. M. J., Lloyd, C. A., & Rowe, K. J. (2008). The impact of leadership on student outcomes: An analysis of the differential effects of leadership types. *Educational Administration Quarterly, 44*(5), 635-674.

Rogers, C. (1954). *Becoming a person.* Martino Fine Books.

Rosenthal, R., & Babad, E. Y. (1985). Pygmalion in the gymnasium. *Educational Leadership, 43*(1), 36-39. https://faculty.darden.virginia.edu/clawsonj/COURSES/DOC_SEM_PEDAGOGY/Carl%20Rogers%20Ch%2013.pdf

Rosenthal, R., & Jacobson, L. (1968). *Pygmalion in the classroom.* The Urban Review.

Salo, P., Nylund, J., & Stjernstrøm, E. (2015). On the practice architectures of instructional leadership. *Educational Management Administration & Leadership, 43*(4), 490-506. https://doi.org/10.1177/1741143214523010

Southworth, G. (2002). Instructional leadership in schools: Reflections and empirical evidence. *School Leadership & Management, 22*(1), 73-92.

Spillane, J. P. (2006). *Distributed leadership.* Jossey-Bass.

Spillane, J. P., Halverson, R., & Diamond, J. B. (2001). Investigating school leadership practice: A distributed perspective. *Educational Researcher, 30*(3), 23-28. https://doi.org/10.3102/0013189X030003023

Stern, J. (n. d.). *Education to save the world website.* Retrieved September 28, 2020, from https://edtosavetheworld.com/resources/

Stern, J., Ferraro, K., & Mohnkern, J. (2017). *Conceptual understanding. Designing lessons and assessments for deep learning. Tools for teaching. Secondary.* Corwin Press.

Timperley, H., Wilson, A., Barrar, H., & Fung, I. (2007). *Teacher professional learning and development: Best evidence synthesis iteration.* Ministry of Education, Wellington, New Zealand.

Tschannen-Moran, M., & Barr, M. (2004). Fostering student learning: The relationship of collective teacher efficacy and student achievement. *Leadership and Policy in Schools, 3*(3), 189–209.

Tschannen-Moran, M., & Gareis, C. R. (2007). Cultivating principals' self-efficacy: Supports that matter. *Journal of School Leadership, 17*(1), 89–114. https://doi .org/10.1177/105268460701700104

UNESCO. (2021). *Education: From disruption to recovery.* https://en.unesco .org/covid19/educationresponse#dura tionschoolclosures

van Bodegom-Vos, L., Davidoff, F., & Marang-van de Mheen, P. J. (2017). Implementation and de-implementation: Two sides of the same coin? *BMJ Quality and Safety, 26*(6), 495–501. https://doi .org/10.1136/bmjqs-2016-005473

van der Merwe, H., &Parsotam, A. (2012). School principal stressors and a stress alleviation strategy based on controlled breathing. *Journal of Asian and African Studies, 47*(6), 666–678.

Wang, V., Maciejewski, M. L., Helfrich, C. D., Weiner, B. J. (2018). Working smarter not harder: Coupling implementation to de-implementation. *Healthcare, 6*(2), 104–107. https://doi.org/10.1016/j .hjdsi.2017.12.004.

Ward, C. J., Fisher, D., Frey, N., & Lapp, D. (2013). *Using data to focus instructional improvement.* ASCD.

Westman, L. (2018). *Student-driven differentiation. 8 Steps to harmonizing learning in the classroom.* Corwin Teaching Essentials Series. SAGE.

Woolley, A. W., Aggarwal, I., & Malone, T. W. (2015). Collective intelligence and group performance. *Current Directions in Psychological Science, 24*(6), 420–424. https://doi .org/10.1177/0963721415599543

Yan, R. (2020). The influence of working conditions on principal turnover in K-12 public schools. *Educational Administration Quarterly, 56*(1), 89–122. https://doi .org/10.1177/0013161X19840391

INDEX

A SAGE Publishing Company

Helping educators make the greatest impact

CORWIN HAS ONE MISSION: to enhance education through intentional professional learning.

We build long-term relationships with our authors, educators, clients, and associations who partner with us to develop and continuously improve the best evidence-based practices that establish and support lifelong learning.

THE PROFESSIONAL LEARNING ASSOCIATION

Learning Forward is a nonprofit, international membership association of learning educators committed to one vision in K–12 education: Equity and excellence in teaching and learning. To realize that vision, Learning Forward pursues its mission to build the capacity of leaders to establish and sustain highly effective professional learning. Information about membership, services, and products is available from www.learningforward.org.

Leadership That Makes an Impact

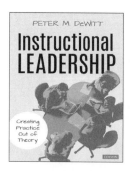

PETER M. DEWITT

This step-by-step how-to guide presents the six driving forces of instructional leadership within a multistage model for implementation, delivering lasting improvement through small collaborative changes.

JOHN HATTIE & RAYMOND L. SMITH

Based on the most current Visible Learning® research with contributions from education thought leaders around the world, this book includes practical ideas for leaders to implement high-impact strategies to strengthen entire school cultures and advocate for all students.

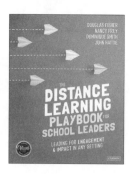

DOUGLAS FISHER, NANCY FREY, DOMINIQUE SMITH, & JOHN HATTIE

This essential hands-on resource offers guidance on leading school and school systems from a distance and delivering on the promise of equitable, quality learning experiences for students.

STEVEN M. CONSTANTINO

Explore the how-to's of establishing family empowerment through building trust, and reflect on implicit bias, equitable learning outcomes, and the role family engagement plays.

MICHAEL FULLAN, JOANNE QUINN, & JOANNE MCEACHEN

The comprehensive strategy of deep learning incorporates practical tools and processes to engage educational stakeholders in new partnerships, mobilize whole-system change, and transform learning for all students.

JOANNE QUINN, JOANNE MCEACHEN, MICHAEL FULLAN, MAG GARDNER, & MAX DRUMMY

Dive into deep learning with this hands-on guide to creating learning experiences that give purpose, unleash student potential, and transform not only learning, but life itself.

DAVIS CAMPBELL & MICHAEL FULLAN

The model outlined in this book develops a systems approach to governing local schools collaboratively to become exemplars of highly effective decision making, leadership, and action.

DAVIS CAMPBELL, MICHAEL FULLAN, BABS KAVANAUGH, & ELEANOR ADAM

As a supplement to the best-selling *The Governance Core*, this guide will help trustees and superintendents adopt a governance mindset and cohesive partnership.

To order your copies, visit **corwin.com/leadership**

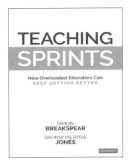

SIMON BREAKSPEAR & BRONWYN RYRIE JONES

Realistic in demand and innovative in approach, this practical and powerful improvement process is designed to help all teachers get going, and keep going, with incremental professional improvement in schools.

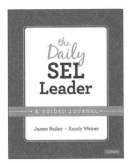

JAMES BAILEY & RANDY WEINER

The thought-provoking daily reflections in this guided journal are designed to strengthen the social and emotional skills of leaders and create a strong social-emotional environment for leaders, teachers, and students.

MARK WHITE & DWIGHT L. CARTER

Through understanding the past and envisioning the future, the authors use practical exercises and real-life examples to draw the blueprint for adapting schools to the age of hyper-change.

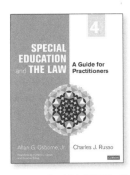

ALLAN G. OSBORNE, JR. & CHARLES J. RUSSO

With its user-friendly format, this resource will help educators understand the law so they can focus on providing exemplary education to students.

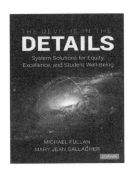

MICHAEL FULLAN & MARY JEAN GALLAGHER

With the goal of transforming the culture of learning to develop greater equity, excellence, and student well-being, this book will help you liberate the system and maintain focus.

TOM VANDER ARK & EMILY LIEBTAG

Diverse case studies and a framework based on timely issues help educators focus students' talents and interests on developing an entrepreneurial mindset and leadership skills.

THOMAS HATCH

By highlighting what works and demonstrating what can be accomplished if we redefine conventional schools, we can have more efficient, more effective, and more equitable schools and create powerful opportunities to support all aspects of students' development.

LYN SHARRATT

Explore 14 essential parameters to guide system and school leaders toward building powerful collaborative learning cultures.

CORWIN